Effective Resources
for
Able & Talented
Children

Barry Teare

Published by Network Educational Press Ltd.
PO Box 635
Stafford
ST16 1BF

First Published 1999
© Barry Teare 1999

ISBN 1 85539 050 7

Barry Teare asserts the moral right to be
identified as the author of this work.

Edited by Gina Walker
Design & layout by
Neil Hawkins of Devine Design
Cover & additional illustrations by
Barking Dog Art, Stroud, Glos.

Printed in Great Britain by
Redwood Books, Trowbridge, Wilts.

Contents

Using this book

This book, *'Effective Resources for Able and Talented Children'*, stands in its own right, but to some extent it is also a companion volume to *'Effective Provision for Able and Talented Children'*, by Barry Teare (Network Educational Press, 1997). In that first book, chapters were devoted to background theory, policy, the target group, identification strategies, school ethos, pastoral care, personnel issues, provision in the classroom, enrichment activities, monitoring and evaluation, and resources. This second book, in Sections One and Two, develops ideas surrounding curriculum provision for able children much further, thereby providing extension to particular chapters of *'Effective Provision for Able and Talented Children'*.

The great majority of this book, though, is devoted to materials that can be used directly with able children (Section Three). This hopefully answers the oft-heard plea from teachers for more ready-to-use resources of this kind. The materials are targeted mainly at Key Stages 2 and 3 of the National Curriculum and P3 to S2 in Scotland. However, chronological age is not a very good guide where able children are concerned, so flexibility is an important consideration.

The materials are grouped into Themes for convenience, but this is only a general indication of use. Some pieces of work could equally well have appeared in other Themes. The chart on page 5 indicates where each piece of work has relevance, and there is additional guidance on cross-referencing within the commentaries at the start of each Theme. These commentaries also provide background thinking to the Themes and indicate how items fit into the requirements of the National Curriculum and the Scottish 5-14 Guidelines, as well as providing for the more general needs of able pupils. This is a very important feature of the book, as interesting and challenging delivery of set content is a key element in providing for able children.

Each piece of work is followed by either a 'solution', or teaching notes, or both. On many occasions there is guidance on the thinking skills involved and the different ways in which the pieces can be used. It is essential to read the teaching notes carefully to get the best out of the materials. Every effort has been made to suggest alternative methods, as variety is tremendously important.

Those who have seen the model for the target group in the author's *'Effective Provision for Able and Talented Children'* will realise that only some of the suggested groups have been catered for in this book. Other children, with physical talents and mechanical ingenuity for example, require suitable opportunities that are beyond the scope of this text. Even so, the materials included here are very varied and they do address the preferred learning styles of many children. Outcomes vary considerably, as is appropriate.

Within Section Three there are eleven important Themes but others could be developed. The pieces can be used directly, or teachers, on some occasions, may wish to make their own amendments to suit local conditions. Whichever is the case, teachers are urged to use these tried and tested materials and enrich the lives of able children.

Use of materials

	Literacy	Word Play	English	Writing	Visual	Subject specific language	History	Geography	Science	Numeracy	Maths	Reading	Group work	Moral ethical	Problem-solving	Decision-making	Information-processing	Logical thought	Codes	Detective work	Alternatives, imagination, creativity	Applicable elsewhere
Carp	✓	✓	✓																			
Ant	✓	✓	✓																			
Lemon Sole	✓	✓	✓	✓																		
The Missing Letter	✓	✓	✓		✓																	
Doing the Proverbial	✓	✓	✓																		✓	
The Full Monty	✓	✓	✓																			
Poetic Licence	✓	✓	✓																		✓	
Depict	✓	✓			✓	✓	✓	✓	✓												✓	✓
Quintessential Qualities	✓	✓	✓			✓	✓	✓													✓	✓
Four	✓	✓				✓					✓											
Mole, Rat, Badger, Toad and Who?	✓		✓	✓								✓									✓	
The Bare Bones	✓		✓	✓								✓	✓								✓	
Tangled Tales			✓	✓								✓	✓								✓	
And That's the End of the Story			✓	✓																	✓	
Straight from the Horse's Mouth		✓	✓	✓			✓							✓							✓	
The Man in the Van			✓	✓																	✓	
Mouthwatering	✓		✓	✓																		
Opening Up a New Chapter	✓		✓	✓									✓								✓	
Acute						✓				✓	✓		✓									
A Calculated Risk						✓				✓	✓		✓								✓	
Board with Numbers?						✓				✓	✓											
In the Balance										✓	✓											
The Year of the Dragon																						
Lucky Programme				✓					✓						✓						✓	
Property To Let									✓						✓	✓					✓	
Professor Malaprop				✓		✓			✓													✓
Ruby Red									✓						✓		✓	✓				
In the Swim															✓	✓	✓					
Field and Track															✓		✓	✓				
Food for Thought	✓							✓							✓	✓	✓	✓				
According to the Book			✓					✓				✓						✓				
Radio Six																		✓				
Lucky the Cat									✓		✓							✓	✓			
Mosaic											✓							✓	✓			
Crosswords		✓	✓																✓			
The Way the Wind Blows		✓	✓				✓							✓	✓	✓			✓		✓	
Decision Makers							✓							✓	✓	✓						
Eyam																						
On the Map					✓												✓					
Seeing is Believing							✓											✓		✓	✓	
According to the Evidence							✓	✓									✓	✓		✓		
An Arresting Problem								✓			✓						✓	✓		✓		
Vital Evidence							✓	✓	✓											✓		
The Question Is				✓			✓	✓													✓	✓
Or							✓		✓												✓	✓
Who Am I?																					✓	✓
Now You See It					✓																✓	✓
Just Imagine							✓	✓	✓					✓							✓	✓

Section One

Ten tools to build a curriculum for the more able

This section will examine:

☞ *the development and expansion of curriculum principles laid down in 'Effective Provision for Able and Talented Children' by Barry Teare (Network Educational Press, 1997)*

☞ *the ways in which the identification of able children informs provision for them*

☞ *how the needs of able children are met through a challenging and well-thought-out curriculum*

☞ *the key role played by the higher-order thinking skills and different forms of differentiation*

☞ *how the views of able children themselves are taken into account*

Introduction

KEY MESSAGE
IT IS IMPORTANT TO ESTABLISH GOOD CURRICULUM PRINCIPLES TO INFORM PROVISION, TO STIMULATE THE WRITING OF APPROPRIATE MATERIALS AND TO PROVIDE A BASE FROM WHICH TO JUDGE THE SUITABILITY OF RESOURCES.

There are various ways of analysing the curriculum needs of able children. Much of the research work done on the left and right sides of the brain, and the practical application of Howard Gardner's theory of multiple intelligences by practitioners such as Alistair Smith, provide the basis for one worthwhile route.

Robert Fisher of the Centre for Thinking Skills at Brunel University has his own taxonomy of thinking skills for the National Curriculum. He sees a number of key qualities as 'providing opportunities for intellectual growth':

awareness	imagination
perseverance	fluency
risk-taking	flexibility
sensitivity	originality
curiosity	elaboration

Two of Fisher's books, *'Teaching Children to Learn'* and *'Teaching Children to Think'* (both Stanley Thornes (Publishers), 1995), are also particularly useful.

Many of the approaches, including the two above, are concerned with good and varied teaching and learning styles for children in general. Much of the thinking has great relevance for able pupils in particular. Despite this overlap, there are particular considerations to take into account when providing specifically for the able and talented.

KEY MESSAGE
MANY TEXTS ON, AND APPROACHES TO, TEACHING AND LEARNING HAVE AN IMPORTANT ROLE TO PLAY BUT, IN ADDITION, THERE ARE SPECIFIC FACTORS TO BEAR IN MIND WHEN DESIGNING A CURRICULUM FOR THE MORE ABLE.

This combination of the general and the specific has proved very helpful in INSET at both primary and secondary levels.

The ten tools

There follows a summary of the 'ten tools', which are each considered in more detail below:

1   The needs of able pupils
2   The characteristics of able pupils
    a. in a general sense
    b. at subject-specific level
3   The sections of the National Curriculum, of the Scottish 5-14 Guidelines, or of any other systems or courses, that encourage enrichment and extension
4   A taxonomy, such as Bloom's, to encourage the higher-order thinking skills
5   Evidence from specialist publications and the OFSTED and Scottish HMI inspection systems
6   Discussion of what makes a piece of work or task difficult and challenging
7   The various types of differentiation
8   Strategies for provision in the classroom specifically, in the school generally, and beyond
9   Surveys of what able children themselves think
10 The range of leisure materials (books, games, etc.) favoured by able children

1:   The needs of able pupils
The list could be very lengthy but some of the important needs of able children are as follows:

1   space to make individual contributions from open-ended situations
2   the opportunity to take risks in an organised way with the facility to fail without threat
3   contact with like-minded people, either peers or adults
4   a fair proportion of teachers' time but deployed differently than for other pupils
5   a good balance of working with urgency and pace, and time to reflect
6   question-and-answer sessions that play to the higher-order thinking skills
7   only as much instruction as is needed, thus allowing the able to interpret what is required for themselves
8   opportunities to develop work further

Effective Resources for Able and Talented Children © Barry Teare (Network Educational Press, 1999)

9 an environment in which alternative methods and alternative answers are encouraged

10 work set in such a way that creativity and imagination are involved extensively

11 Schemes of Work that recognise appropriate starting points and subsequent steps rather than 'blanket' instructions for everybody

12 an appreciation that ability is not always matched by social and emotional development

13 a variety of teaching styles to accommodate the individual learning needs of different pupils

2:   The characteristics of able pupils

a.   In a general sense

There are many examples of good checklists of general characteristics of able pupils: for example, in *'Able Pupils: Practical Identification Strategies'* (NACE/DfEE Second Edition, 1996).

These checklists are normally used to help teachers to identify able pupils. They should also be employed to help inform the curriculum and resources. If, for example, the checklist includes a reference to 'ability to deal well with abstract tasks' then there is a clear pointer to the need to include such tasks in the programme for able pupils: for example, algebra in maths and proverbs in English.

b.   At subject-specific level

Checklists of characteristics in particular curriculum areas have more obvious practical possibilities. An example for English is given below.

Able children:

1 listen with a high level of concentration and understanding to varied and complex speech

2 use originality in the choice of the spoken word

3 express a point of view assuredly, fluently, persuasively and with appropriateness to different audiences

4 show agility and quickness in discussion, responding sensitively and convincingly to the views of others

5 take a leading role in oral work, initiating, sustaining and developing dialogue

6 enjoy playing with language especially puns, nuances and word play

7 perform well when working in the abstract, either understanding difficult concepts or using forms such as metaphor and proverbs

8 see links and connections in unusual ways

9 read aloud previously unseen texts fluently and with meaning

10 read, with understanding, an increasing range and complexity of texts, often displaying a huge appetite for books

11 become frustrated quickly with the limitations of books designed for the peer group

12 demonstrate an unusually sensitive response to literature, appreciating language, structure and presentation, and showing awareness of alternative interpretations

13 display a high level of technical ability in their writing, using accurate punctuation and a range of grammatical constructions

14 express outcomes in their writing in an unusual way, creating impact and maintaining the interest of the reader

15 display an extensive vocabulary, orally and within written work

16 show a high level of appreciation for different audiences in the appropriateness of structure, language and length used in written work

17 make good use of previous knowledge and past experience to inform new work

18 develop interesting and unusual ideas from stimuli for creative writing

As with general checklists, subject-specific checklists help to identify able children, but, again, such lists should also inform curriculum provision. It would be perverse to do otherwise.

KEY MESSAGE
THE CHECKLISTS OF CHARACTERISTICS OF ABLE PUPILS BOTH AT A GENERAL LEVEL AND AT SUBJECT LEVEL ARE NOT ONLY VALUABLE TO THE PROCESS OF IDENTIFICATION BUT TO THE PROVISION OF A SUITABLE CURRICULUM AND RESOURCES.

3: Sections of curriculum guidelines that encourage enrichment and extension

Many teachers in England, Scotland and in English-speaking schools in Europe complain that the content and accompanying detailed instruction within which they have to work restricts the use of resources for able pupils. When one looks at Science in the National Curriculum, for example, the information is very lengthy and detailed, and the content is daunting.

One of the great challenges to teachers, however, is to take content over which they do not have control and deliver it in a challenging and enjoyable way. It must be remembered that even before the days of the National Curriculum and Scottish 5-14 Guidelines there was considerable concern about the provision for able children. The problem, then, goes deeper than just the constraints of such systems. It is more about an attitude of mind, though volume of content and lack of time have been damaging.

Careful inspection of the National Curriculum shows that all subject areas include phrases and statements that open the door to enrichment and extension for able pupils, normally through addressing higher-order thinking skills. This was a theme explored in Section One of *'Effective Provision for Able and Talented Children'* (Network Educational Press, 1997). Further examples are given below.

> *They should be encouraged to respond imaginatively to the plot, characters, ideas, vocabulary and organisation of language in literature. They should be taught to use inference and deduction.*
>
> KS2, AT2 English

> *... make conjectures and hypotheses, designing methods to test them, and analysing results to see whether they are valid.*
>
> KS3 and KS4, AT1 Mathematics

> *... use scientific knowledge and understanding to turn ideas suggested to them, and their own ideas, into a form that can be investigated.*
>
> KS3, AT1 Science

> *... consider the effectiveness of a product, including the extent to which it meets a clear need, is fit for purpose, and uses resources appropriately.*
>
> KS2, Design and Technology

> *... analyse and evaluate interpretations.*
>
> KS3, History

> *... analyse and evaluate the evidence, draw conclusions and communicate findings.*
>
> KS3, Geography

> *... develop strategies for dealing with the unpredictable.*
>
> KS3 and KS4, Modern Foreign Languages

Similarly, when one examines the Scottish 5-14 Guidelines, opportunities can be identified. Sections on 'Catering for the Needs of Individual Pupils' look at programmes for pupils beyond Level E and give advice on forms of differentiation that are appropriate. Again some examples are given.

> *Differentiation is achieved by a combination of different levels of text, task and support.*
>
> Modern Foreign Languages

> *... linguistic resourcefulness ... imaginative versatility ...*
>
> English Language

> *Thinking: for example, speculating; hypothesizing; discovering; reflecting; generalizing; synthesizing; classifying; evaluating.*
>
> English Language

> *... apply a problem-tackling process in relevant situations.*
>
> Personal and Social Development

> *... initiate, organise and complete tasks involving others.*
>
> Personal and Social Development

> *... consider, select and organise materials and media and develop knowledge of techniques, processes and skills, appropriate to the activity and to the individual's stage of development, in a learning environment which stimulates awareness and imagination.*
>
> Art and Design within Expressive Arts

> " *... reach new understandings and appreciations of self, others and the environment through imaginative dramatic experience.* "
>
> Drama within Expressive Arts

> " *... recognise situations involving moral conflict, show awareness of alternative viewpoints and be able to offer a personal opinion, backed by reasons.* "
>
> Religious and Moral Education

> " *... are inventive and imaginative in exploring patterns and relationships in number and shape and in searching for problem-solving strategies.* "
>
> Mathematics

> " *... decide on appropriate strategies, procedures, sources of information, evidence and resources/equipment to carry out an investigation or experiment, justifying choices and monitoring for possible unfairness or bias.* "
>
> Science within Environmental Studies

> " *... make predictions about the outcomes of particular design decisions, using knowledge and information gained in several different contexts.* "
>
> Technology within Environmental Studies

> " *... offer increasingly sophisticated explanations for findings.* "
>
> Social Subjects within Environmental Studies

KEY MESSAGES

HAVING TO DELIVER TOO MUCH CONTENT IS NOT HELPFUL, BUT CAREFUL EXAMINATION OF PROGRAMMES OF STUDY PROVIDES SUITABLE OPPORTUNITIES FOR ENRICHMENT AND EXTENSION FOR ABLE PUPILS.

AFTER THE REVISION OF THE NATIONAL CURRICULUM THAT IS TAKING PLACE AT THE TIME OF WRITING, THE WORDING POST-2000 MAY CHANGE SLIGHTLY OR IT MAY REMAIN EXACTLY THE SAME. WHAT WILL NOT CHANGE IS THE NEED TO EXPLORE CAREFULLY ANY SET OF CURRICULUM GUIDELINES TO FIND AND TO USE OPPORTUNITIES FOR ENRICHMENT AND EXTENSION. INDEED, THE SPIRIT OF THE REVISION APPEARS TO BE LEADING TO GREATER ENCOURAGEMENT OF DIFFERENTIATION AND OF TARGETING APPROPRIATE WORK FOR ABLE PUPILS.

4:   A taxonomy to encourage higher-order thinking skills
The Concise Oxford Dictionary defines a 'taxonomy' as 'a scheme of classification'. Robert Fisher's example has already been mentioned (see page 7). Perhaps the most famous example is Bloom's Taxonomy of Thinking Skills.

> **synthesis**
>
> **evaluation**
>
> **analysis**
>
> **application**
>
> **comprehension**
>
> **knowledge**

This is not a strict hierarchy, as one cannot say, for instance, that there is a definite progression from evaluation to synthesis. However, the thinking skills can be seen as falling into three levels.

Knowledge and comprehension are the lower-order skills, even though they are vital to the learning process. Remembering is important but it has obvious limitations. Even so, memory work can be made creative by adopting strategies such as those suggested by Tony Buzan in his excellent book *'Use Your Memory'*, revised edition (BBC Books, 1995). These methods allow imaginative approaches that link the right and left sides of the brain.

Application is a middle-order thinking skill, and allows useful transferability to take place.

The three higher-order thinking skills are analysis, evaluation and synthesis - the last encouraging children to take data, views and opinions from many sources and create something new with much of themselves personally involved in the process.

Susan Winebrenner, in her book *'Teaching Gifted Kids in the Regular Classroom'* (Free Spirit Publishing Inc.), adapted Bloom's Taxonomy to include definitions, trigger words and products. The trigger words are particularly helpful. Alongside 'synthesis' we see triggers such as 'compose', 'design', 'hypothesise', 'construct' and 'rearrange the parts'. These are the opportunities that able children need regularly, and not just 'once in a blue moon'. Much educational research has shown that the higher-order thinking skills are not used enough, either in pieces of work or in question-and-answer sessions.

The University of Western Sydney has produced a simplified Bloom's Taxonomy in the form of a house with a three-storey intellect - gathering, processing and applying. Whichever version is used, Bloom's Taxonomy can make a valuable contribution to the planning of a curriculum for the more able.

> ## KEY MESSAGE
> ### IN THE CLASSROOM, IT IS IMPORTANT TO ENCOURAGE THE USE OF HIGHER-ORDER THINKING SKILLS REGULARLY, TO PROVIDE GOOD CURRICULUM OPPORTUNITIES FOR ABLE CHILDREN.

5:   Evidence from specialist publications and inspection systems

The educational world moves at a fantastic pace. The rate of change and the number of initiatives over recent years have been formidable. Teachers have found it difficult to keep abreast of developments. One initiative is soon superseded by another and stops being 'flavour of the month'. One of the unfortunate results of this situation is that good advice in past reports and publications has been neglected. Time is always a major problem, but if teachers are able to revisit earlier publications they should find that it pays dividends.

In the Cockcroft Report *'Mathematics Counts'* (HMSO, 1982), many observations and recommendations were included in the findings. Two, which are of particular significance for able pupils, encouraged the use of mathematical language and the acceptance of alternative methods of working. There were also sections of advice on 'provision for high-attaining pupils' and 'provision for pupils where attainment is very high'.

'Better Mathematics' (HMSO, 1987) was described as a curriculum development study based on the 'Low Attainers in Mathematics Project'. Even so, it contains a superb set of 'ingredients' for able pupils under the heading 'What Makes a Rich Mathematical Activity?' (Interestingly, the word 'mathematical' could be removed and it would apply to many other areas of the curriculum.)

- It must be accessible to everyone at the start.
- It needs to allow further challenges and be extendible.
- It should invite children to make decisions.
- It should involve children in speculating, hypothesis making and testing, proving or explaining, reflecting, interpreting.
- It should not restrict pupils from searching in other directions.
- It should promote discussion and communication.
- It should encourage originality/invention.
- It should encourage 'what if' and 'what if not' questions.
- It should have an element of surprise.
- It should be enjoyable.

What a superb list!

There are divided opinions about the advantages and disadvantages of the inspection systems in England and Scotland. The findings of individual reports may well be open to dispute and debate. However, when the results of a large number of inspections are collected together and summarised it is profitable to look at comments that occur many, many times in relation to provision for able pupils. Such comments include 'too tightly-prescribed tasks' and 'over-directed teaching'. Publications such as the twelve booklets comprising *'OFSTED - A Review of Inspection Findings 1993/4'* (HMSO, 1995) have contributions to make in a curriculum for the more able.

6:   What makes a piece of work or task difficult and challenging
Many teachers, when asked what should be done about able pupils, would include in their answers the suggestion that more difficult and challenging work should be set. This is fine as far as it goes but it does beg the question of what it is that makes a task more difficult and challenging. This could be a useful INSET exercise for departments or groups of teachers to carry out.

A number of suggestions were teased out in *'Effective Provision for Able and Talented Children'* (Network Educational Press, 1997), after consultations with specialists in a variety of curriculum areas.

Once teachers have such a list of ideas, they should build them into a curriculum for the more able whilst, at the same time, being careful about their inclusion for the less able.

7:   The various types of differentiation

Good use of differentiation is vital in a curriculum for the more able. Readers would be well advised to familiarise themselves with two texts in particular:

- *'Differentiation: a Practical Handbook of Classroom Strategies'*, Chris Dickinson and Julie Wright (NCET, 1993)
- *'Effective Learning Activities'*, Chris Dickinson (Network Educational Press, 1996).

Differentiation techniques are vital for able pupils in any education system. The following sections apply equally to both England and Scotland. Many of the comments have been drawn from the Scottish 5-14 Guidelines, as this is one of the strengths of those documents. They have as much relevance for an English audience.

Differentiation by outcome or response

This is perhaps the most widely used of all forms of differentiation. The same material or stimulus is used for all pupils or, alternatively, the same tasks are set for everybody in the group. Differentiation is achieved by individuals answering at their own levels of ability so that very different outcomes result from the same task or piece of work.

This method works best where the tasks are open-ended, so that pupils have the chance to make something of their personal responses. A major advantage of this form of differentiation is that pupils do not have to be grouped first.

However, be aware that some advisers and inspectors are a little uneasy if the process is used too much and especially where the tasks are not sufficiently open-ended. This is because it is possible that the teacher has not thought through what he or she is doing and is simply setting the same task without a strategy behind it.

Differentiation by resource or text

This method is based upon the fact that some pupils are capable of working with more advanced resources than others. Pupils may be answering the same basic question, but using differing levels of materials upon which to base their answers. Easier texts have less prose and more illustrations, are less dense and use restricted vocabulary and concepts. For the more able, the vocabulary should be more advanced and the ideas expressed in more complex ways.

In history and geography, for instance, one can visualise a range of texts on the same basic information. In modern foreign languages, too, some pupils could be presented with much more detailed and complex materials.

Because of major differences in the ways in which pupils can work, we need to provide a wide variety of resources.

In *'Effective Learning Activities'*, Chris Dickinson advocates the separation of content from tasks. This provides a flexibility that facilitates differentiation by resource.

Differentiation by task

Here a variety of tasks are provided that cover the main content area, in order to provide for the range of individual pupils in the group. One particular consideration is the starting point. More able children could start 'further along the road'. Another important factor is the number of steps to be followed. The less able the child, the smaller the incremental steps need to be. The more able the child the bigger the gaps can be, and therefore the fewer steps that need to be incorporated into the planning.

One technique is to have different cards, worksheets or exercises for different groups of pupils. Some teachers worry about the social implications of handing different pieces of paper out to different children. It is perhaps worth reflecting that much more damage can be done by facing children with material that is beyond them, or by frustrating and boring the more able by not giving them sufficient challenge.

Another application is through group work. Some schools use 'rolling activities' in which different stages of a project are handled by different ability-based groups, depending upon the difficulty of the task involved. The following comment from the Scottish 5-14 Guidelines for Environmental Studies supports this approach to differentiation:

> *... by organising and structuring collaborative group tasks to allow pupils to contribute, each according to his or her different abilities.*

A third technique to achieve differentiation by task involves work sheets that get progressively more difficult. The early tasks are much easier, although that is as far as some children get. The later tasks are much more difficult and are only tackled by able pupils who have raced through the earlier questions. Some teachers find this more acceptable, as the same sheets are given to everybody. The danger is that too much time could be wasted at the start for the more able.

Differentiation by dialogue

This is a term the author first encountered in the work of Chris Dickinson. The most important resource for any child is not paper or electric, but human. Differentiation by dialogue places emphasis on the role of the teacher and the talking that takes place between teacher and pupils. There are various aspects of differentiation by dialogue.

The vocabulary and complexity of language used should vary for different children. The less able child may well require a detailed explanation in simple language. The more able pupil requires a verbal dialogue at a more sophisticated level. All children need appropriate feedback within the dialogue.

The skilled manager of the classroom prompts and encourages pupils with comments suitable to the ability of each child and the degree of progress being made.

Differentiation by support

This approach is linked to differentiation by dialogue, and is based upon the notion that some pupils need more help than others to complete the work set. The amount and degree of help provided can be differentiated to meet the needs of individual pupils.

This support can be provided by the teacher or by other adults. An obvious example would be the help given by a classroom assistant to a child with learning difficulties. The support could come from other pupils or indeed from hardware and information technology. A child under the Code of Practice may require a laptop computer. An able pupil could be supported by an independent learning package. It is worth noting that children of all abilities deserve and need teachers' support, but that the nature of that support should vary.

There is an interesting description of differentiation in the environmental studies section of the Scottish 5-14 Guidelines:

> *...by gradually withdrawing teacher support from pupils, so that they are encouraged to show increased independence in their learning and to exercise greater responsibility for the pace and structure of their work.*

Differentiation by pace
Some children need to move forward very gradually or they become confused. Many able pupils are able to sustain a much quicker programme and they become frustrated if the pace is not strong enough. Even simple tasks become more difficult if they have to be achieved within a limited time.

Lesson planning can then be differentiated in terms of how many and how quickly tasks are to be completed. Urgency and greater pace are key ingredients to satisfy the needs of able pupils.

Differentiation by pace can be interpreted in two different ways. In linear-based subjects such as mathematics and modern foreign languages, it could involve more able pupils going through a set course much more quickly, getting progressively further ahead. This is often referred to as acceleration or fast-tracking. In other subjects, such as the humanities, this would be inappropriate. Here differentiation by pace would involve more able children working more quickly, but into enrichment or extension tasks rather than progressing onto the next unit. Clearly this second interpretation could also be applied to the linear-based subjects.

Differentiation by content
Some pupils create time by their quick and successful mastery of 'the basics' to look at content beyond the norm. This is an important use of time, rather than the waste of doing 'more of the same'. The flavour of this form of differentiation is captured in the following comment from the Scottish 5-14 Guidelines for mathematics:

> *Mathematics can be enriched, both through further study of content already explored, and through investigating aspects of mathematics not included in the minimal targets.*

Differentiation by independence or responsibility
This fits alongside some of the issues raised in differentiation by support. Within the differentiation section of the Scottish 5-14 Guidelines for English language, some interesting ideas are developed. Peer assessment and self-assessment are recommended

as part of the teaching and learning process. It is suggested that able pupils are more capable of such forms of assessment:

> *In a similar way the teacher may gradually free such pupils to make choices about how to learn and sometimes what to learn.*

KEY MESSAGES

APPROPRIATE AND SKILFUL USE OF DIFFERENTIATION IS VITAL TO THE WELL BEING OF ABLE PUPILS.

DIFFERENTIATION SHOULD NOT BE LEFT TO CHANCE BUT SHOULD, RATHER, BE WRITTEN INTO SCHEMES OF WORK.

MORE THAN ONE TYPE OF DIFFERENTIATION CAN BE EMPLOYED WITHIN THE SAME TASK OR PIECE OF WORK.

8: **Strategies for provision in the classroom specifically, the school generally, and beyond**

Such strategies could include:

1   Schemes of Work for all sections of all syllabuses, which provide, in a planned way, for the most able in the group by one or more methods of enrichment and/or extension
2   a grouping policy that centres upon the needs of individuals
3   use of the different forms of differentiation - pace, task, dialogue, support, outcome, resource, content, responsibility
4   differentiated homeworks
5   clubs at lunchtime or after school, covering academic as well as other activities
6   a loan service of enrichment materials from the library or elsewhere
7   special competitions
8   as wide an extra-curricular programme as can be resourced
9   visits from poets, writers, actors, dancers, etc. into school
10 use of the expertise and interests of able pupils to help deliver the curriculum
11 celebration of all areas of the curriculum on a regular basis
12 establishing a school newspaper and/or subject-based magazines
13 activities weeks to allow more unusual areas to be explored, and longer blocks of time for activities
14 enrichment sessions during the school day
15 mentoring by either a similarly-talented adult or a suitably encouraging adult
16 cluster activities with other schools
17 taking advantage of LEA-based activities, where appropriate and available
18 use of masterclasses at the local university
19 co-operating with appropriate older groups
20 joint action with the local community
21 consideration of the enrichment activities provided by outside associations and organisations, both subject-based and more general

Effective Resources for Able and Talented Children © Barry Teare (Network Educational Press, 1999)

KEY MESSAGES

ITEMS 1-4 IN THE LIST ABOVE ARE ABOUT PROCEDURES. IT IS IMPORTANT TO ESTABLISH PROCEDURES TO CONVERT POLICY INTO PRACTICE AND PROVISION, THUS EMBEDDING PRINCIPLES INTO DAY-TO-DAY WORK.

ITEMS 5-15 SHOW SOME OF THE MANY WAYS IN WHICH SCHOOLS CAN PROVIDE RICH AND DIVERSE OPPORTUNITIES. SCHOOLS WHERE 'THERE IS NEVER A DULL MOMENT' OFFER AN ENVIRONMENT OF OPPORTUNITY THAT IS STIMULATING TO ALL PUPILS BUT ESPECIALLY TO THE ABLE.

SCHOOLS DO NOT HAVE TO MAKE ALL THE PROVISION IN-HOUSE. IT IS JUST AS IMPORTANT TO FACILITATE OPPORTUNITIES BEYOND THE SCHOOL (AS INDICATED IN ITEMS 16-21).

THE YOUNGER THE CHILD, THE MORE DIFFICULT IT IS TO USE 'OUTSIDE' PROVISION. THEREFORE, FOR YOUNGER PUPILS, THERE IS A HEAVIER RESPONSIBILITY UPON THE SCHOOL ITSELF AND ESPECIALLY UPON THE CLASSROOM TEACHER.

9:   Surveys of what able children themselves think

In recent years there has been a growing desire to talk to pupils, to hear their views and to try to appreciate what school is like from their perspective. Clearly this is a valuable tool to use with able children, many of whom are very articulate and perceptive. It is not the easiest of ventures to undertake, as some of the results may be uncomfortable to handle. One could argue that running such a survey was an indication of the confidence and maturity of the school.

Some of the areas that could be included in such a survey are listed below.

Ten teasers

1   Which subjects are most enjoyable? Why?
2   What are your preferred teaching styles?
3   Was the work in a particular year challenging enough?
4   Which activities are boring?
5   Is homework of real value?
6   Is it best to work on your own, in pairs, in small groups, as a class, in a group of the teacher's choosing, in a group of your own choosing?
7   What factors motivate you to do well?
8   What factors impede your progress?
9   Is there sufficient space for you to use your own ideas, imagination, creativity?
10   Is the atmosphere in school conducive to high achievement?

10:   The range of leisure materials favoured by able children

When one works with able children in school or on enrichment courses it is fascinating to see what it is that most interests them during their leisure time. Not all of the activities on which they spend time are necessarily of interest to the teacher but there are many clues to be followed.

While working on Saturday Clubs for the National Association for Gifted Children, the author would look specifically at what participants were buying or asking for as presents. When he heard that '*The Warlock of Firetop Mountain*' had sold out three times in the Manchester Grammar School bookshop, then he felt it might be worthwhile getting hold of a copy. When a child who produced the most incredible answers in enrichment activities was intrigued by a puzzle from Shafir Games called 'Old McDonald's Farm', it seemed sensible to have a look at the puzzle.

More recently, when asking children on enrichment courses at Kilve Court in Somerset what they enjoyed reading, the author was intrigued to see how popular are the *'Horrible Histories'* by Terry Deary - even with boys who are supposedly not reading much. An analysis of the features of those books could be very informative.

In conclusion

- We need well-thought-out theory to inform the provision for able pupils.

- Once the needs and characteristics of able children have been identified, they need to be fed into the curriculum.

- Using the higher-order thinking skills with sufficient frequency is particularly important in curriculum provision for the more able.

- A real understanding, and then application, of the forms of differentiation is essential.

- There is a wide range of appropriate strategies that can be employed, and together they make a rich provision.

- Once the curriculum principles are understood, it makes it much easier to develop and purchase effective resources for able and talented children.

Section Two

Being resourceful

This section will examine:

- ☞ what constitutes a resource for able pupils

- ☞ how able pupils are taken into account within Schemes of Work

- ☞ checking out texts for use with able children

- ☞ the value of specially constructed materials

- ☞ the short term and long term goals in the preparation of resources

- ☞ the features of enrichment materials, task and activities

- ☞ considerations involved when writing your own enrichment materials

- ☞ a new selection of commercially produced resources

1:   What constitutes a resource for able pupils?

Riches are for spending.

Francis Bacon Essays, *'Of Expense'*

A register of resources

All of these are of value in provision for able children:

1   the teacher(s)
2   ancillary help, such as classroom assistants
3   parental expertise, both at home and used in school
4   visiting poets, writers, dancers, speakers, dance troupes, etc.
5   peer expertise
6   contact with like-minded individuals, whether adults or children
7   a school policy that sets out the principles, procedures and practices, in a coherent way
8   departmental or curriculum area policies that apply the whole-school policy in subject-specific ways
9   a school ethos that encourages high achievement
10 an environment that stimulates the mind, the imagination and the individuality of able pupils
11 a pastoral system that looks to *all* the needs of able pupils
12 a flexible assessment system
13 dedicated finance
14 time
15 space

16 physical resources
17 material resources that are appropriate for a curriculum for the more able
18 the Internet
19 availability of activities through co-operation with other schools
20 LEA or area-based enrichment activities
21 masterclasses
22 schools of excellence, orchestras, youth theatres, etc.
23 opportunities in the local community
24 carefully prepared visits to places of interest

KEY MESSAGE
THERE ARE MANY FACETS TO THE MEANING OF 'RESOURCES FOR ABLE PUPILS'.
THE SUM OF THE WHOLE IS GREATER THAN THE PARTS.

Many of the resources listed above are self-explanatory. Those who wish to examine issues surrounding policies, school ethos, finance, and so on, in more detail are directed to 'Effective Provision for Able and Talented Children', by Barry Teare (Network Educational Press, 1997). The purpose of this volume is to concentrate more upon material resources and provision, but it is worthwhile to develop two areas further here.

The teacher

The most valuable resource of all is human.

> *A teacher is better than two books.*
>
> German proverb

What qualities in a teacher are of greatest value to the able child? Each person would probably produce a different list, but many of the following might figure prominently.

Teachers should be:

enthusiastic	On its own, enthusiasm is not sufficient but it is a very powerful and influential factor.
inspirational	Teachers should inspire through example and personal qualities.
humble	Teachers should accept that they do not have all the answers, all the time, and that some children are more capable than they are.
purposeful	All that is done in the classroom should be for a good reason.
possessing a sense of humour	So many able children have a quirky sense of humour themselves.
knowledgeable	They don't need to know it all, but able children become disappointed if there are too many gaps.
challenging	There needs to be rigour, pace and urgency.

flexible	Able children need to be allowed to use their individual talents through alternative answers.
imaginative/creative	Able pupils tend to respond well to unusual presentation.
forward-looking	Teachers should aim for progress in conjunction with the thoughts of the child.
risk-taking	Teachers should encourage children to see how far they can go, but in a caring and organised way.
facilitating	Good guidance and advice should be offered, without domination or over-direction.
responsive	'Signals' from the able child need to be understood, and helpful feedback given.
interesting	Teachers cannot enrich children unless they are enriched themselves.

KEY MESSAGE
THE TEACHER IS BY FAR THE MOST IMPORTANT RESOURCE FOR ALL CHILDREN, INCLUDING THE MOST ABLE.

Time

There is a time for all things.

English proverb

'If we only had time...' is a constantly heard plea, in many areas of life. Let us examine some particular time difficulties that teachers experience in relation to provision for able pupils, in the table overleaf.

Three dimensions of time

'Dimension'	Response
1 There is no time, due to the demands of National Curriculum, the Scottish 5-14 Guidelines etc.	This is difficult, especially in subjects like science. However, able pupils often complete the 'basic tasks' quickly and well. They *produce* time for themselves. What is then important is how that time is used. Doing more of the same, or being engaged in lengthy but undemanding tasks, is a *waste* of time. This space could be used for enrichment and extension. In addition, with some creative thinking, items that *have* to be covered can be dealt with through more imaginative materials. In Section Three of this book (see page 39) there are many examples of pieces of work that answer sections of syllabuses, but in challenging, creative and imaginative ways.
2 Teachers are so overburdened with work and a plethora of initiatives that there is no time to develop enrichment materials for the able.	This is not an easy situation to overcome especially as there is a dearth of good commercial materials. Co-operation and sharing seem the most sensible ways forward. Groups of teachers, either within a school or further afield, could produce an item each and then have common use of the pooled resources. Some management teams may feel that it is necessary to allow time on INSET days for the development of materials, or to arrange staff release for this purpose. A third approach is to use curriculum insight to exploit existing resources for new uses.
3 Blocks of time within school are insufficient to allow certain types of activities to be completed.	Activities weeks and occasional suspensions of the normal timetable provide longer blocks of time. Able pupils can also be brought together for enrichment activities within the normal school day.

KEY MESSAGES

TIME PROBLEMS DO POSE DIFFICULTIES BUT THEY CAN BE RESOLVED, AT LEAST TO SOME DEGREE, BY A FLEXIBLE APPROACH, CO-OPERATION AND CAREFUL PLANNING.

SMALL, INCREMENTAL STEPS WILL LEAD TO GOOD PROGRESS.

Effective Resources for Able and Talented Children © Barry Teare (Network Educational Press, 1999)

2: Able pupils and Schemes of Work

If the daily diet for able children is to be improved then Schemes of Work are an important means of delivery.

Two key considerations

- Writing details into Schemes of Work helps to bridge the gap between policy and practice.

- A disciplined approach involves a process by which issues are addressed in the classroom as a matter of course.

Points to address

Time
- Given that able pupils may not need as long to complete tasks, what plans are made for the remaining time?

Links with the National Curriculum
- Are Levels that are beyond the norm for the children's chronological age accessible in the work?
- Have pupils likely to work beyond Level 8 been taken into account?
- Do you have a workable and effective description for 'Exceptional Performance'?
- Has work at the next Key Stage been considered?

Links with the Scottish 5-14 Guidelines
- Are Levels that are beyond the norm for the children's chronological age accessible in the work?
- Have the activities for pupils beyond Level E and Standard Grade been taken into account?
- Has the advice on differentiation in many of the guidelines been considered?
- Have the characteristics of pupils operating beyond Level E, described in many of the guidelines, been taken into account?

Differentiation
- Have the appropriate type(s) of differentiation been identified?
- Is this section just a 'sop' or is the thinking relevant and sharp?
- Are there links with other parts of the Scheme of Work, such as Time and Resources?

Purposes
- Have skills and concepts relating especially to able pupils been given sufficient weighting?
- Are the higher-order thinking skills, and their 'trigger' words (see page 13), in evidence?

Progression
- Are all the pupils going to start at the same point?
- Is there the facility for able pupils to be involved in fewer steps?

Resources
- Has consideration been given to the availability of more complex and challenging material?

Assessment
- Will credit be given for unusual but perceptive responses?
- Is there sufficient flexibility in the marking scheme?

> **KEY MESSAGES**
>
> **SCHEMES OF WORK ARE AN IMPORTANT PROCEDURE FOR MAKING SURE THAT POLICIES ON ABLE AND TALENTED CHILDREN ARE CONVERTED INTO GOOD PRACTICE AND PROVISION.**
>
> **'ROME WAS NOT BUILT IN A DAY' BUT A SUSTAINED, ALBEIT GRADUAL, PROGRAMME WILL HAVE A MAJOR IMPACT ON DAY-TO-DAY PROVISION.**

3: Checking out texts for able pupils to use

Most publishers make a series of claims about the texts they produce for schools. It has to be said that some of the activities ostensibly designed specifically for able pupils do not live up to expectations. Teachers may well wish to follow the procedure below.

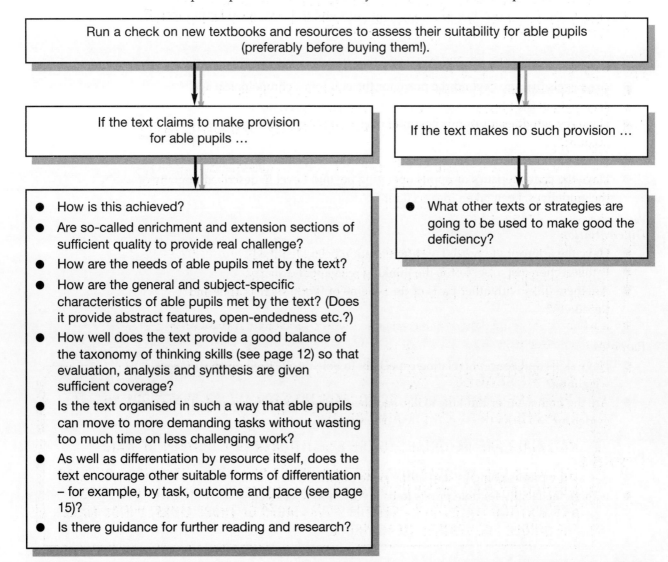

Run a check on new textbooks and resources to assess their suitability for able pupils (preferably before buying them!).

If the text claims to make provision for able pupils …

If the text makes no such provision …

- How is this achieved?
- Are so-called enrichment and extension sections of sufficient quality to provide real challenge?
- How are the needs of able pupils met by the text?
- How are the general and subject-specific characteristics of able pupils met by the text? (Does it provide abstract features, open-endedness etc.?)
- How well does the text provide a good balance of the taxonomy of thinking skills (see page 12) so that evaluation, analysis and synthesis are given sufficient coverage?
- Is the text organised in such a way that able pupils can move to more demanding tasks without wasting too much time on less challenging work?
- As well as differentiation by resource itself, does the text encourage other suitable forms of differentiation – for example, by task, outcome and pace (see page 15)?
- Is there guidance for further reading and research?

- What other texts or strategies are going to be used to make good the deficiency?

Effective Resources for Able and Talented Children © Barry Teare (Network Educational Press, 1999)

4: The value of specially constructed materials

Enrichment and extension materials created specifically for more able pupils are invaluable because:

- official reports and inspection feedback still comment that able pupils are not given appropriate tasks often enough
- there is a shortage of good materials for the able produced commercially
- teachers can best understand principles through specific examples of materials and children's responses to them
- hard-pressed teachers welcome the availability of suitable resources
- working with the resources makes the classroom practitioner more receptive to the accompanying theory and general principles
- such materials provide exemplars so that models and stimuli are available for those who wish to adapt and write their own

Even so, there are some doubts and worries:

- 'cold' materials do not work
- even potentially brilliant materials can be ruined by poor use
- it is difficult to work with other people's materials - teachers do not feel ownership
- approach and attitude are critical, and therefore INSET is more important than the materials themselves

Ways of dealing with the doubts:

- clear and detailed notes for teachers could be written to accompany the materials
- the materials could be used as an integral part of INSET
- materials could be adapted and changed to suit individual schools and/or classrooms
- teachers could write their own materials so that the problem of ownership is overcome (see page 31)

5:   Short term and long term goals

Both long term and short term targets have to be born in mind when considering provision for more able pupils.

Long term targets

All Schemes of Work should include enrichment and extension tasks that develop naturally from the foundation.

Advantages

+ When a child completes the work set for the whole class, quickly and well, there are challenging and interesting materials readily available.
+ The additional work is not artificial but forms a natural extension to the topic of the lesson, or the foundation.

Problems

− This involves suitable enrichment and extension tasks for every unit of every Scheme of Work, for every class in the school.
− The time and effort involved are considerable.
− This has to be seen as a gradual programme to be completed over time. In the meantime, the short term goals can be considered.

Short term targets

Individual items should be provided, not necessarily based on the foundation, which improve the quality of tasks set and reduce the mismatch between able pupils and their programmes of work.

Advantages

+ Progress can be made gradually.
+ The target is more feasible for individual teachers in the classroom.
+ There is an improvement in the appropriateness of work set.

Problems

− This is a second best policy.
− Enrichment and extension materials are not as meaningful when they move away from the focal point of the lesson.

6:   Features of enrichment materials, tasks and activities

Enrichment

Enrichment should comprise a planned pattern of activities across the curriculum to supplement exciting provision during normal lessons, and takes place within an ethos of achievement and participation.

For able pupils, this could involve:

1   unusual elements that are not normally covered
2   competitions - school-based, regional or national
3   an opportunity to look more broadly at a unit of work
4   an opportunity to borrow materials as well as books from the library
5   rich strands brought together in extra-curricular programmes
6   a chance to share interests and passions with others of like mind
7   a celebration of a particular area of the curriculum
8   an enjoyable, but very demanding challenge
9   working with talented adults
10 clubs and societies that go beyond the normal knowledge base
11 cluster activities with pupils from other schools
12 concentration upon the higher-order thinking skills
13 letting loose creativity and imagination
14 participation at a high level of skill and expertise
15 exploring alternative routes and methods
16 sufficient space to experiment
17 a curriculum varied enough to reach the interests of all children
18 working brilliantly as a team
19 using their own expertise to benefit others
20 pushing forward their own personal bests
21 learning something new - perhaps far from normal experience
22 sharing a sense of beauty and wonder
23 achieving a goal through determination and persistence over a period of time
24 the excitement of working at pace and with urgency
25 benefiting from the inspiration and enthusiasm of a peer or adult
26 being allowed to make individual progress
27 time to think and reflect
28 ringing the changes to keep work fresh and appealing
29 taking advantage of LEA-organised activities
30 a suspension of the normal timetable
31 masterclasses
32 'finding themselves'
33 intriguing presentation of material to capture the imagination and to stimulate
    exciting and varied responses

> ## KEY MESSAGES
> ENRICHMENT CAN INVOLVE A LARGE NUMBER OF CONTRASTING METHODS.
>
> THE MORE METHODS USED, THE RICHER THE PROGRAMME, THE MORE VARIED
> ARE THE OPPORTUNITIES FOR ABLE CHILDREN.

These various interpretations of enrichment can then lead to the use of particular
materials and resources.

Some features of enrichment materials

No one task or material can hope to meet all demands at the same time but, collectively, enrichment resources should do the following:

1 provide a diverse curriculum
2 promote individuality of response
3 maintain a good balance between closed and open-ended materials
4 satisfy very different time spans
5 suit the characteristics and needs of able pupils
6 involve information-processing, problem-solving and decision-making
7 operate at able pupils' 'frontiers of knowledge'
8 encourage creativity, imagination and lateral thinking
9 provide opportunities for logical thinking, deduction and inference
10 answer necessary content but in a challenging way
11 encourage role-play and empathy
12 use varied inputs and varied outcomes
13 open up opportunities for further development and research
14 maintain a good balance of pace/urgency and reflection
15 give a sense of satisfaction, fulfilment and enjoyment

> **KEY MESSAGE**
> AN UNDERSTANDING OF THE ASPECTS OF ENRICHMENT, OF THE FEATURES OF ENRICHMENT MATERIALS, AND OF THE PRINCIPLES BEHIND A CURRICULUM FOR THE MORE ABLE, TOGETHER WITH AN APPRECIATION OF THE DEMANDS OF SYLLABUSES AND COURSES, CAN LEAD TO THE PROVISION OF RESOURCES THAT ARE APPROPRIATE FOR ABLE AND TALENTED CHILDREN.

Visits

Visits to museums, concerts, exhibitions, natural features, fairs, and so on, are part of the 'enrichment picture'. To get maximum benefit, there needs to be careful preparation and appropriate follow-up. Ironically, some of the best locations have a limited range of educational worksheets and materials as far as the able pupil is concerned. The Natural History Museum, for example, is a wonderful venue with excellent exhibits, brilliant halls and exciting experiences. Even so, the worksheets are the same for everybody.

> **KEY MESSAGE**
> EVEN WHEN A VENUE HAS GREAT EDUCATIONAL VALUE, DIFFERENTIATED RESOURCES TO ACCOMPANY THE VISIT MAY NEED TO BE DEVELOPED.

7: Writing and producing your own materials

Some years ago, various groups of teachers worked together to produce excellent materials, normally for local use. These included:

- the Birmingham Progress Team
- the MAC materials in Newcastle
- Croydon LEA
- social and economic history units in Avon
- problem-solving materials in Lancaster

Unfortunately, such writing collaborations have become far less frequent as a result of increased pressure upon teachers and the decline of LEA-based curriculum groups. Individual schools could create their own materials, though cluster activities involving several schools would help to share the load.

If a school wishes to create its own enrichment and extension materials, what are the decisions that have to be made? The first six considerations below are concerned with the nature of the materials themselves, while the remaining points are more to do with their production, distribution and evaluation.

A dozen decisions

1: *Principles*
Underlying curriculum principles have been discussed in Section One. The most critical decision of all is to decide which features will underpin the materials: for example, they could be based upon a problem-solving model, or use of higher-order thinking skills, and so on. How will the materials work in terms of the National Curriculum or the Scottish 5-14 Guidelines?

2: *Size of the target group*
Some very difficult or complex materials may be aimed at small groups of children: for example, those used in the mathematics masterclasses run under the auspices of the Royal Institution. Others could be used with much wider populations, especially where open-ended materials are concerned. This decision is linked to the group's/school's philosophy on what constitutes ability and how many able children there are, together with a view on which areas of human activity should be included in the provision. (See Section Three in *'Effective Provision for Able and Talented Children'* by Barry Teare (Network Educational Press, 1997).)

3: *Age*
How are the materials to be designated in terms of the age of the children? Curriculum guidelines help to some extent but even Key Stages and Levels are moveable. The problem is that chronological age does not have much relevance where able children are concerned. A degree of flexibility is required alongside guarded guidance for teachers.

4: *Subject base*
The decision here is whether the materials are to slot easily alongside curriculum areas - English, mathematics, science, geography - or whether they are intended to be cross-curricular. The specialities of the personnel in the writing team may well have an important influence.

5: *When and where are the materials to be used?*

There are a number of possibilities, including:

- normal lessons
- differentiated homeworks
- enrichment sessions
- withdrawal groups
- individual study
- loans from the library

6: *Length*

The able child often finishes up with a few minutes to spare, having completed the set work quickly. Some materials for short spans of time would then be helpful. Some writers have devised programmes of extended work to go over several weeks. There is merit in a mixture of items of various lengths so that a number of different circumstances are satisfied.

7: *Authorship*

How many people will be involved in the actual writing? Will they write as individuals, pairs or a group? Committees are notorious for the quality of joint reports but individuals need to work within some agreed parameters.

8: *Editorial decisions*

Not all materials turn out well. Some enthusiastic participants find the task very difficult. Who makes the decisions about whether a particular piece is to be developed and used? Do all the members of the group vote or is somebody designated 'editor' with the power of a final decision?

9: *Production*

How and where will the materials be produced? What standards are to be set for the finished product? How important will presentation be?

10: *Availability*

Are the materials for:

- individual teachers
- groups of teachers or departments
- the school generally
- a cluster of schools
- interested parties?

11: *Teacher guidance*

The writers will understand the purpose of their materials and how they should be used to good effect. How are the context and understanding to be conveyed to other users? One way is to include teaching notes. Even then 'cold' materials often do not 'come alive' - their potential may not be seen. INSET to accompany the materials is very valuable and may make all the difference. Good responses from children are also powerful tools to demonstrate the value of the materials.

12: Evaluation

Evaluation can take place at different stages:

- during trialling of the materials to see whether changes should be made
- when the materials are put into proper use, for this adds alternative methods and interpretations as different teachers bring their own expertise and methodologies to bear
- when they are tried in a new context such as an enrichment session

It is therefore sensible to include evaluation sheets with enrichment materials. A discussion involving a number of teachers who have used the resources is likely to be more effective, of course, but suitable opportunities for such meetings may be difficult to find.

8: Commercially produced materials

Even though there is a shortage of good enrichment materials on the market, there are some notable exceptions. They come from diverse quarters and they are not always to be found in conventional education catalogues.

On INSET run by the author, teachers have always been keen to look at materials suitable for able and talented children, and to take details about those that are of particular interest. There are constant requests for extensive book lists. Section Nine in *'Effective Provision for Able and Talented Children'* has proved popular for its description of commercially produced materials, some of a rather unusual nature.

In the same spirit, here is a new and additional 'catalogue' of materials acquired by the author.

Texts

Alistair Smith, *'Accelerated Learning in the Classroom'* (Network Educational Press, 1996)

Alistair Smith, *'Accelerated Learning in Practice'* (Network Educational Press, 1998)

Chris Dickinson, *'Effective Learning Activities'* (Network Educational Press, 1996)

Steven Bowkett, *'Imagine That'* (Network Educational Press, 1997)

Pat O'Brien, *'Teaching Scientifically Able Pupils in the Secondary School'* (National Association for Able Children in Education, sponsored by Glaxo Wellcome, 1998)

Pat O'Brien, *'Teaching Scientifically Able Pupils in the Primary School'* (National Association for Able Children in Education, sponsored by Glaxo Wellcome, 1998)

Deborah Eyre, *'Teaching More Able Pupils'* (National Association for Able Children in Education, with funding from the National Lottery, 1998)

Catherine Clark and Ralph Callow, *'Educating Able Children'* (NACE/David Fulton Publishers, 1998)

Susan Leyden, *'Supporting the Child of Exceptional Ability'*, second edition (NACE/David Fulton Publishers, 1998)

Geoff Dean, *'Challenging the More Able Language User'* (NACE/David Fulton Publishers, 1998)

Joan Freeman, *'Educating the Very Able'* - research evidence from home and abroad (OFSTED/The Stationery Office, 1998)

Tony Buzan, *'Use Your Memory'*, latest edition (BBC Books, 1995)

Robert Fisher, *'Teaching Children to Think'* (Stanley Thornes (Publishers), 1995)

Robert Fisher, *'Teaching Children to Learn'* (Stanley Thornes (Publishers), 1995)

Michael Dansel, *'50 Best Memory Methods and Tests'* (Foulsham, 1997)

Word games, word power, word play

A.R. Melrose, *'The Pooh Dictionary'* (Methuen, 1995)

Steve Palin, *'A Dissimulation of Birds'* - a wonderful illustrated 'collective nouns of birds' (Minerva Press, 1998)

Jeffrey Kacirk, *'Forgotten English'* - a rollicking guide to archaic words and their definitions (New York: William Morris and Company, 1997)

'The Oxford Dictionary of New Words' - as a contrast to the previous reference! (Oxford University Press, 1997)

Jon Scieszka and Lane Smith, *'Squids will be Squids'* - another brilliant book from these authors; this time 'Fresh Morals: Beastly Fables' (Viking, 1998)

Daniel Mermet and Henri Galeron, *'Lulubird Euchres the Noodleheads'* - nonsense words that convey more meaning than normal words! (Harlin Quist, 1998)

Richard Whiteley, *'Letters Play'* - a treasure trove of word games and ideas (Robson Books, 1995)

Literature - loosely speaking

Adrian Mourby, *'Whatever Happened To ...?'* - 'The Ultimate Sequels' from Radio 4 and Winner of the Sony Silver Award for Creative Writing; the humour will appeal to older children (Souvenir Press, 1997)

Frank Barrett, *'Where was Wonderland?'* - a traveller's guide to the settings of classic children's books (Hamlyn, 1997)

Picture Books

David Macauley, *'Rome Antics'* - a heady mix of architecture, storytelling, spatial awareness, imagination, mystery and word play (Dorling Kindersley, 1997)

Colin Thompson, *'How to Live Forever'* (Red Fox, 1998)

Colin Thompson, *'The Tower to the Sun'* (Random House, 1996)

Colin Thompson, *'The Paradise Garden'* - these three books from Colin Thompson are visually stunning and intriguing, with layers of meaning (Jonathan Cape, 1998)

Quentin Blake, *'Clown'* - a challenge to write your own text (Red Fox, 1998)

Michele Coxon, *'Who will Play with Me?'* - try writing a two-way story of your own (Happy Cat Books, 1995)

Quentin Blake, *'The Story of the Dancing Frog'* - another one for text interpretation; see what Prue Goodwin makes of it in *'Great Books for The Literacy Hour and Beyond'* (see below) (Red Fox, 1996)

BIG picture books

Korky Paul and Valerie Thomas, '*Winnie the Witch*' (Oxford University Press, 1998)

Korky Paul and Valerie Thomas, '*Winnie in Winter*' (Oxford University Press, 1998)

Ruth Brown, '*A Dark Dark Tale*' - visually dramatic, especially at this size (as are the two references above) and full of opportunities for text exploration (Andersen Press, 1998)

Children's reading books

Children's literature is alive and well, despite the gloomy comments about reading. As well as the classics and the modern classics, there are some wonderful recent titles. Try the following, and many, many others.

Philip Pullman, '*Northern Lights*' (Scholastic, 1995)

Philip Pullman, '*The Subtle Knife*' (Scholastic, 1997)

Gillian Cross, '*Pictures in the Dark*' (Oxford University Press, 1996)

Anne Fine, '*The Tulip Touch*' (Puffin, 1996)

J.K. Rowling, '*Harry Potter and the Philosopher's Stone*' (Bloomsbury, 1997)

J.K. Rowling, '*Harry Potter and the Chamber of Secrets*' (Bloomsbury, 1998)

Theresa Tomlinson, '*Meet Me by the Steelmen*' (Walker Books, 1997)

Malorie Blackman, '*Lie Detectives*' (Scholastic, 1998)

Reading guides

Michael Rosen and Jill Burridge, '*Treasure Islands 2*' (BBC Books, 1995)

Wendy Cooling, '*The Puffin Literacy Hour Booklist*' (Puffin/W.H. Smith)

'*Great Books for the Literacy Hour and Beyond*' (Random House Children's Books)

'*The Children's Book Handbook*' (Young Book Trust, 1998)

'*Off the Shelf*' (Book Trust Scotland)

'*100 Best Books, 1996*' (Young Book Trust, 1996)

'*100 Best Books, 1997*' (Young Book Trust, 1997)

'*100 Best Books, 1998*' (Young Book Trust, 1998)

Mathematics - or with that sort of angle

Wilson Ransome, '*Number-Cell Challenge*' - a collection of ingenious number puzzles (Tarquin, 1996)

Magdalen Bear, '*Days, Months and Years*' - a perpetual calendar for the past, present and future (Tarquin, 1996)

Heather McLeavy, '*The Knots Puzzle Book*' - looking at knots in a different way; a collection of interesting mathematical ideas (Tarquin, 1994)

Gerald Jenkins and Magdalen Bear, '*Sundials and Timedials*' (Tarquin, 1987)

Reg Sheppard and John Wilkinson, '*Strategy Games*' - a wealth of activities involving games (Tarquin, 1989)

Ian Stewart, '*The Magical Maze*' - two videos and a booklet covering the brilliant Royal Institution Christmas Lectures, 1997 (BBC Publications, 1997)

Adam Case, '*Who Tells the Truth?*' (Tarquin, 1996)

David Blatner, '*The Joy of π*' - certainly joy to those who love number but produces a shudder with others! (Penguin, 1997)

Carol Vorderman, '*How Mathematics Works*' - a beautifully presented book containing a large number of practical experiments (Dorling Kindersley, 1996)

Jon Scieszka and Lane Smith, '*Maths Curse*' - simple examples but a wonderful text to emulate (Puffin, 1998)

Brian Bolt, '*A Mathematical Pandora's Box*' - another in the series; the title tells you all you need to know! (Cambridge University Press, 1993)

Christopher Clapham, '*Oxford Concise Dictionary of Mathematics*' - excellent in stimulating greater use of mathematical language (Oxford University Press, 1996)

'*The 24 Game*' - popular for stimulating mental mathematics at many levels of difficulty (Suntex International, 1993)

Miscellaneous and unusual dice, educational suppliers, shows, exhibitions - who knows where they might lead?

Science - but certainly not pure

Gerald Jenkins and Magdalen Bear, '*The Sun, Moon and Tides*' - model-building book (Tarquin, 1995)

Borin Van Loon, '*DNA: The Marvellous Molecule*' - another model-building book (Tarquin, 1990)

BNFL and Royal Botanic Gardens, Kew, '*Looking for Links*' - book and video investigating the connections between the natural and made worlds (Resources for Learning Ltd., 1995)

BNFL, '*Energy - Picture Card Game*' - visual presentation for young children; what else could you do with them? (Resources for Learning Ltd., 1993)

Melvyn Bragg, '*On Giants' Shoulders*' - the book of the BBC Radio 4 series on great scientists and their discoveries (Hodder and Stoughton, 1998)

BNFL, '*Energy Jingles*' - rhymes, limericks and verses; perhaps to suit a different preferred learning style (Resources for Learning Ltd.)

Brenda Keogh and Stuart Naylor, '*Starting Points for Science*' - the concept cartoons, as seen on the London Underground, especially for children who have a visual preference (Millgate House Publishers, 1997)

Dava Sobel, '*Longitude*' - solving 'the thorniest scientific dilemma of the day' (Fourth Estate Ltd., 1995)

Gary Larson, '*There's a Hair in my Dirt*' - an eccentric and brilliantly funny look at ecology (Little, Brown and Company, 1998)

BNFL/Royal Microscopical Society, '*The Young Detectives*' - video, incident wall map, photocards, computer program and teacher's book, which 'not only helps teachers to understand the remit of Sc1 but, by offering a hypothetical 'whodunnit', opens to pupils the excitement of carrying out investigations for themselves' (Resources for Learning Ltd., 1997)

Effective Resources for Able and Talented Children © Barry Teare (Network Educational Press, 1999)

Russell Stannard, '*The Time and Space of Uncle Albert*' (Faber, 1989)

Russell Stannard, '*Black Holes and Uncle Albert*' (Faber, 1991)

Russell Stannard, '*Uncle Albert and the Quantum Quest*' - these three fairy stories from Russell Stannard help explain the principles of modern physics to children (Faber, 1994)

Humanities - any time, any place

Paul Warren, '*Caleb Beldragon's Chronicle of the Three Counties*' - an imaginary land that should inspire children to create their own (Heinemann, 1995)

Terry Deary, '*Horrible Histories*' - very popular with many able pupils (Scholastic)

'*London on Playing Cards*' - a chance for creative mapwork (Intercol, 1989)

Dyan Sheldon and Gary Blythe, '*The Garden*' - a beautifully illustrated picture book, which could inspire local history projects (Red Fox, 1995)

Religion and philosophy - something to think about

Andrew Matthews and Allan Curless, '*Cat Song*' - a picture book with 'a truly original view of creation' (Red Fox, 1996)

Robert Martin Walker, '*Politically Correct Parables*' - an unusual sense of humour from an ordained Methodist minister (Harper Collins, 1996)

Richard Fox, '*Thinking Matters*' - a collection of stories, based upon Matthew Lipman's work, which are meant to encourage children to think for themselves (Southgate Publishers, 1996)

Matthew Lipman, '*Harry Stottlemeier's Discovery*' - this, and many other texts, are used for the Philosophy for Children courses (Institute for the Advancement of Philosophy for Children, Montclair State College, 1982)

Imagination/visual

Chris McEwan, '*Eye See, Do You See?*' - a fantastical other world, full of paradox and illusion (Orchard Books, 1995)

Mike Wilks, '*The Ultimate Spot-the-Difference Book*' - a visual adventure to test the powers of observation to the very limit (Penguin Books, 1997)

The Templar Company, '*Mythical Mazes*' - a collection of beautifully illustrated labyrinths associated with legends (Templar Publishing, 1996)

James Gurney, '*Dinotopia: The World Beneath*' - 'the balance of science and nature created by James Gurney's imagination' (Dorling Kindersley, 1995)

Guy Billout, '*A Question of Detail*' - brilliant visual images and concepts (Harlin Quist, 1998)

Codes

Jeff Hawtin, '*Secret Messages*' (Tarquin, 1990)

Gerald Jenkins and Ann Wild, '*Be a Codebreaker*' (Tarquin, 1997)

John Foley, '*The Guinness Encyclopedia of Signs and Symbols*' - a treasury of ideas to follow up (Guinness Publishing, 1993)

Detective materials

(See *'The Young Detectives'* under Science)

David Parkinson and Guy Parker-Rees, *'Pinkerton Inks - The Case of the Pigeon's Pyjamas'* - a light-hearted picture book for younger children (Oxford University Press, 1996)

An attractive set of small books from Lagoon:

Nick Hoare, *'Murder on the Riviera Express'* (Lagoon, 1996)

Nick Hoare, *'Murder in Manhattan'* (Lagoon, 1996)

Nick Hoare, *'Death After Dinner'* (Lagoon, 1996)

Nick Hoare, *'Murder at Thrippleton Hall'* (Lagoon, 1996)

Simon Melhuish and Jenny Lynch, *'Sixty-Second Murder Puzzles'* (Lagoon, 1997)

Jigsaws/wooden puzzles

'WASGIJ' - three available so far; this is jigsaw backwards and the puzzle is constructed from the position of one or more characters in the picture (Falcon Puzzles)

'Scroll Puzzles' - a range to suit different ages, right up to executive examples, which are used 'by management training schools, universities and large multinational companies'; the puzzles are made of very odd shapes and the finished product is far from the norm (Active Education, Kentisbeare, Devon)

In conclusion

- People are the most important resource for able children and there are key qualities that they need to display.

- Procedures such as Schemes of Work and checking texts help the provision of a suitable curriculum for the more able.

- Resources for able pupils can not only help hard-pressed teachers but also give those teachers ideas to develop themselves.

- The long-term goal has to be the inclusion in all Schemes of Work of enrichment and extension tasks that stem from the subject matter of the lesson.

- Familiarisation with the different forms of enrichment and the features of enrichment materials helps to provide effectively and successfully for able children.

- Writing your own materials is not easy or without time and effort but it has many advantages once key decisions have been taken.

- Good commercially produced materials, designated for the specific use of able children, are in short supply but there are many other resources to consider from less obvious sources.

Section Three

Resources for enrichment and extension

Theme One: *Literacy*

Literacy has always been a key issue in education and many arguments have raged over standards. Key Stages 1 and 2 of the National Curriculum now see greater emphasis upon a literacy strategy, which, in turn, will have implications for teaching at the secondary stage. Even before the recent developments there was a need to find enjoyable and challenging ways of presenting material to able children, while at the same time promoting a good standard for all pupils.

The National Literacy Strategy has heightened the tension between these two tasks. Some people have expressed concern that the tight structure of the Literacy Hour, which requires some 40 minutes to be devoted to whole class teaching, might be at the expense of appropriate provision for the most able. The framework document for the implementation of the National Literacy Strategy in the classroom is very prescriptive, and some teachers may feel that they have a straitjacket to contend with, just as some perceived the National Curriculum as being restrictive. The interests of able children will not be well served by unnecessary time spent on concepts and skills that they have already mastered, but which need further practice by other members of the class.

Just as with the National Curriculum, there is plenty of scope within the Literacy Framework for enrichment and extension. Of course, texts for whole class use will need to be chosen very carefully. Word games can be used to lighten the delivery of grammatical awareness: for example, adverbs and adverbial phrases are explored through puns in *Tom Swifties* (see Enrichment Activities in '*Effective Provision for Able and Talented Children*', Barry Teare (Network Educational Press, 1997)).

In the Scottish 5-14 Guidelines, too, there are key phrases to exploit in the description of work beyond Level E:

> *a cognitive grasp of quite sophisticated ideas and linguistic concepts ... linguistic resourcefulness ... imaginative versatility*

Punctuation has a detailed programme in the Literacy Framework. Theme Eight: **Codes** (see page 167) provides a reminder of an exercise called *A Capital Idea* included in '*Effective Provision for Able and Talented Children*'. Other forms of punctuation could be dealt with in a similar way, thus combining essential content with challenging and enjoyable presentation.

The vocabulary extension section of the Literacy Framework provides excellent opportunities for able pupils. Homonyms are introduced at the end of Year 3. *Carp* (page 44) is an enjoyable activity to stretch able pupils in English. It extends their vocabulary while at the same time playing to word humour, which is a characteristic of many able children.

Ant (page 46) is included to help distinguish between homophones, i.e. words with common pronunciations but different spellings and/or meanings (Year 5, Term 2). In this case, both spelling and meaning are different. *Lemon Sole* (page 48) extends this work by words, spelled and sounding the same, but with three different meanings.

Strong references are made to the use of a range of dictionaries. Lessons based upon this can soon become very mechanical and pedestrian. *The Missing Letter* (page 50) is one way of encouraging the use of a thesaurus through a very challenging piece of work. Lipograms are exercises in which the pupil is required to rewrite a short passage without using a certain 'banned' letter, but keeping the meaning as close as possible to the original. Splendid examples are quoted in the 'Absent Friends' section of *'Letters Play'*, Richard Whiteley (Robson Books, 1995). *The Missing Letter* is a particularly demanding example of the lipogram because the 'e' is banned!

Proverbs are particularly valuable in work with able children, as they are abstract - they contain symbolic meanings, expressing a general truth in a short, pithy saying. This plays to one of the characteristics of many able children. Proverbs often portray a humorous image, which appeals to the sense of humour of many able pupils. Despite being unfashionable for some years, proverbs have continued to be valued in some schools, and it is particularly pleasing to see them included in the Literacy Framework (Year 6 Term 2). *Doing the Proverbial* (page 52) provides a variety of activities including some that involve visual presentation, which fits the preferred learning style of some children.

The use of rich and diverse vocabulary is a key ingredient in both the National Curriculum and the Scottish 5-14 Guidelines. The English language section of the Scottish 5-14 Guidelines looks to teachers who will:

> *...help pupils to develop confidence and pleasure in their own use of language.*
>
> *...make all pupils aware of the importance of language.*

The National Curriculum is more specific, with reference to:

> *...discussion of more imaginative and adventurous choice of words.*
>
> KS2 AT1
>
> *Their interest in words should be extended by the discussion of language use and choices.*
>
> KS2 AT3
>
> *...how usage, words and meanings change over time.*
>
> KS3 and KS4 AT1
>
> *...the coinage of new words and origins of existing words.*
>
> KS3 and KS4 AT1

Effective Resources for Able and Talented Children © Barry Teare (Network Educational Press, 1999)

The Literacy Framework contains a vocabulary extension section on a term-by-term basis. The many, many references include:

> ...to understand how new words have been added to the language.
>
> Year 6 Term 1
>
> ...to understand that the meanings of words change over time.
>
> Year 6 Term 2
>
> ...to experiment with language, e.g. creating new words, similes and metaphors.
>
> Year 6 Term 3

The Full Monty (page 55) is offered as an enjoyable way of exploring new words and phrases in our language, or changes in their use.

Another way of looking into the richness of language is an exploration of the many literary terms that can enliven our writing, reading and speaking. Poetic Licence (page 60) looks at fifteen such terms in a practical way, looking for examples either in picture books or in the immediate environment.

CARP

The picture above illustrates a word that has two quite different meanings. A clue to this word could be: **'A freshwater fish complains'**

Your task

Can you identify the fifteen words below that have a double meaning (at least) from the clues given?

1   A quick form of abstinence. (4)

2   A type of transport is a way to keep fit. (5)

3   A poor tennis performance suggests romance. (4)

4   Idle away time on a natural satellite. (4)

5   Close examination of a small opening in the skin. (4)

6   In electronics a conductor leads to questioning closely. (5)

7   A small shovel has an exclusive use in the newspaper industry. (5)

8   A period of development on a raised platform. (5)

9   Pester a burrowing animal. (6)

10 A sum of money used as sports equipment. (4)

11 Musicians in a thin flat strip. (4)

12 A natural water source in good health. (4)

13 Prevent with a large solid piece of wood or stone. (5)

14 To rush for a punctuation mark. (4)

15 Soft fine hair moves to a lower level. (4)

CARP

Solution

1 fast

2 train

3 love

4 moon

5 pore

6 probe

7 scoop

8 stage

9 badger

10 bail

11 band

12 well

13 block

14 dash

15 down

ANT

Illustrated above is an ant. A word that sounds similar but which is spelled differently is 'aunt'. The two of them could be defined by the joint clue: **'The female relative of a small insect'**

Your task

Below there are fifteen other clues to pairs of words that sound similar but which are spelled differently. See if you can identify them.

1   Two of a fruit.

2   A worker who is under-aged and underground.

3   The location of a view.

4   The notice of a trigonometric function.

5   Given instruction in a tense way.

6   A small room to exchange for money.

7   A coin is transmitted to another place.

8   An actual cylindrical frame or spool.

9   Precipitation controls the horse.

10   To stay in one place in expectation of a measure.

11   Frail for seven days.

12   The outer skin of a reverberatory sound.

13   To direct one's attention to good fortune.

14   A large form of fireplace.

15   Grass that produces edible grain in instalments.

ANT

Note to teachers

The following pairs of words sound similar: allowances need to be made for dialects.

Solution

1   pair and pear

2   minor and miner

3   site and sight; scene and seen

4   sign and sine

5   taught and taut

6   cell and sell

7   cent and sent

8   real and reel

9   rain and rein

10   wait and weight

11   weak and week

12   peel and peal

13   look and luck

14   great and grate

15   cereal and serial

LEMON SOLE

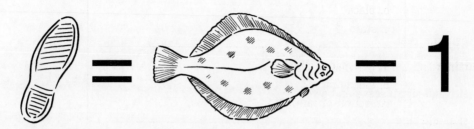

Some words have at least three different meanings, but the word has the same spelling in each case. In the following clue, there are three meanings of the word 'sole' - the fish, the 'only' purpose, and the sole of Philip's shoe.

> *Philip went into the fishmongers and chose two fillets for the evening meal. This was not the only purpose for his visit to the shops. He also wanted to take his shoes in for repair.*

Your tasks

Below there are ten more clues, each involving a word with three different meanings but the same spelling. Try to identify the word in each case.

1. The judging panel was quick to see the place that had a small stain on it.
2. The newspaper clipping contained some damaging comments upon the state of the track in that particular section of the railway system.
3. A large number of people accept that their destiny has been decided by a chance selection.
4. Inexperienced players sometimes play shots very close to the flag itself when a safer option would be better. They are envious of the judgement of more established players.
5. The builder put a fastening on the gate, then ate his food quickly so that he could dash off.
6. After the sixth ball, the bowler had finished his work. He looked across to the captain to see where he was to field.
7. Having climbed up the rock face, the explorer could see the animal. There was only one boney plate on the head, but many on its tail. It looked small against the vastness of the cliff.
8. The ambassador had been in her present position for five years. First thing each morning she dealt with the most important letters. Then, before her other duties, she sprinkled seed onto the bird table, which was fastened to a stake in the ground outside her office window.
9. Close to the battle lines, many soldiers put up an appearance that they were not frightened. When an attack was to be launched, however, they would look anxiously ahead.
10. Paul's body shook with laughter when he thought of the problems he and his friend had experienced putting up the picture. Anyway, now the job was done, they were free to play a game of snooker.

Further work

✎ Write your own clues, constructed as those above, based upon the words:

GAME   FOOT   COUNTER   TOAST   TRAIN

✎ Find other words with three meanings and write clues to illustrate them.

LEMON SOLE

Solution

1	**Spot:**	a. see b. place c. stain
2	**Cutting:**	a. newspaper clipping b. damaging c. section of railway
3	**Lot:**	a. large number b. destiny c. chance selection - drawing lots
4	**Green:**	a. inexperienced b. golf green c. envious
5	**Bolt:**	a. fastening b. eat quickly c. dash off
6	**Over:**	a. cricket over b. finished c. across
7	**Scale:**	a. climb up b. boney plates on an animal c. relative size
8	**Post:**	a. position b. letters c. stake
9	**Front:**	a. battle lines b. put up an appearance c. ahead - in front
10	**Frame:**	a. body b. picture frame c. frame of snooker

THE MISSING LETTER

E E E E E

This challenge involves a **lipogram** - a piece of writing composed of words to avoid the use of a particular letter.

Below is the first paragraph from the Sherlock Holmes' story *'The Blue Carbuncle'.*

> *I had called upon my friend Sherlock Holmes upon the second morning after Christmas, with the intention of wishing him the compliments of the season. He was lounging upon the sofa in a purple dressing-gown, a pipe-rack within his reach upon the right, and a pile of crumpled morning papers, evidently newly studied, near at hand. Beside the couch was a wooden chair, and on the angle of the back hung a very seedy and disreputable hard felt hat, much the worse for wear, and cracked in several places. A lens and a forceps lying upon the seat of the chair suggested that the hat had been suspended in this manner for the purpose of examination.*

Your tasks

✍ If you had to rewrite the passage above with one of the five vowels forbidden, which one would you choose and why? (Assuming that you wanted to make your task as easy as possible!)

✍ Rewrite the passage above avoiding the use of the letter 'e'. Try to keep to the meaning as closely as possible. If you think that this is impossible use the letter 'e' only when you have to, but work hard to make 'e' 'the missing letter' that does not appear at all.

THE MISSING LETTER

A possible solution

Below is one possible solution to the lipogram problem based upon 'The Blue Carbuncle' extract, avoiding the use of the letter 'e'. This 'solution' was done at speed, and is, of course, one of very many possible answers.

> *I paid a visit upon my companion, S. H., two days post Christmas, a.m., to wish him 'Happy Christmas'. I found him lounging upon a sofa in a burgundy wrap, a rack to hold his smoking tools to his right, and a stack of morning journals in disarray S.H. had just put down from scanning, by him. By his couch was a chair of wood, and hanging from its back was a much worn and shabby hard fabric hat with cracks in it, a magnifying glass and small tongs lying on this chair implying that this hat was hung in this way to scan it.*

DOING THE PROVERBIAL

Most of us are aware of the traditional meanings of well-known proverbs. Below there are fifteen proverbs described in rather strange terms.

1   The quality of the meal is not improved by the number of culinary experts.

2   Allow dormant animals to tell untruths.

3   In bad weather a drink is welcome.

4   A group of lions arrives before autumn.

5   Recreational activities for small rodents in the absence of the gamekeeper.

6   No arithmetic until the shells crack.

7   A dressing for meals is equally suitable for male and female.

8   You need more than one container for the hen's products.

9   A dead man's legacy means the use of scales.

10   A sum of money enables a person to make a musical request.

11   Good weather encourages work with the grass.

12   Sewing for an hour avoids longer shifts.

13   There are ten pence pieces in the dark sky.

14   One creature regrets an alarm clock in the trees.

15   Beef could be like arsenic next door.

Your tasks

✍ Work out the fifteen proverbs described above. (For example, 'Increased workforce in the electricity industry' could mean 'Many hands make light work'.)

✍ Devise your own strange descriptions for these proverbs, and for some others.

✍ Try illustrating proverbs with diagrams. (For example, the illustration at the top of the page is for 'Many hands make light work'.)

✍ Make up some new proverbs of your own.

DOING THE PROVERBIAL

A selection of proverbs

A stitch in time saves nine.	Better late than never.
Let sleeping dogs lie.	It's easy to be wise after the event.
Learn to walk before you run.	What's sauce for the goose is sauce for the gander.
A new broom sweeps clean.	Honesty is the best policy.
One swallow does not make a summer.	He who pays the piper calls the tune.
Still waters run deep.	Any port in a storm.
Make hay while the sun shines.	Truth will out.
Too many cooks spoil the broth.	Enough is as good as a feast.
Every cloud has a silver lining.	A rolling stone gathers no moss.
No news is good news.	Pride goes before a fall.
Practice makes perfect.	The early bird catches the worm.
One good turn deserves another.	One man's meat is another man's poison.
Empty vessels make most noise.	Waste not, want not.
A word is enough to the wise.	It's an ill wind that blows nobody any good.
Don't look a gift horse in the mouth.	A little knowledge is a dangerous thing.
All good things come to an end.	Don't put the cart before the horse.
Necessity is the mother of invention.	Every why has a wherefore.
Half a loaf is better than none.	Strike while the iron is hot.
All that glitters is not gold.	Absence makes the heart grow fonder.
Where there's a will there's a way.	Once bitten, twice shy.
Forbidden fruit tastes sweetest.	More haste, less speed.
Don't count your chickens until they are hatched.	Actions speak louder than words.
A miss is as good as a mile.	While the cat's away the mice will play.
Cut your coat according to your cloth.	Do as you would be done by.
A creaking gate hangs longest.	Don't put all your eggs in one basket.
We never miss the water till the well runs dry.	Cross the stream where it's shallowest.
It takes two to quarrel.	You can't have your cake and eat it.
Don't cross the bridge until you come to it.	Familiarity breeds contempt.
People who live in glass houses shouldn't throw stones.	The grass is greener on the other side of the fence.

DOING THE PROVERBIAL

Teaching notes

Proverbs tend to have gone out of fashion, which is a pity, as any form of word play is valuable and instructive. The abstract quality of proverbs makes them particularly appealing to able children. It is therefore good to see that proverbs are now included in Year 6 of the National Literacy Framework. *Doing the Proverbial* attempts to set proverbs in an interesting and imaginative context with a strong fun element.

An important decision for the teacher is how much assistance should be given. A great deal will depend upon the background information the pupils hold. Pupils with a good working knowledge could be asked to identify the proverbs without any help. Other pupils could be given the fifteen answers in mixed order and asked to match them with the clues. Another possibility is to give a list of 30 proverbs or more, fifteen of which are the ones described in the exercise.

The fifteen proverbs described are:

1   Too many cooks spoil the broth.

2   Let sleeping dogs lie.

3   Any port in a storm.

4   Pride goes before a fall.

5   While the cat's away the mice will play.

6   Don't count your chickens until they are hatched.

7   What's sauce for the goose is sauce for the gander.

8   Don't put all your eggs in one basket.

9   Where there's a will there's a way.

10   He who pays the piper calls the tune.

11   Make hay while the sun shines.

12   A stitch in time saves nine.

13   Every cloud has a silver lining.

14   The early bird catches the worm.

15   One man's meat is another man's poison.

THE FULL MONTY

Our language continues to develop and to grow. New words and phrases are added and, in other cases, there are new meanings for established words and phrases. The title of this exercise, *The Full Monty*, is described in *'The Oxford Dictionary of New Words'* as meaning 'everything that is necessary or appropriate - the works'. The record-breaking film of the same name illustrated a particular example of 'the works'!

Below there are twenty new words and phrases. Three of them are misleading in that they are misquoted. For each of the twenty decide whether the word or phrase is correct or not. Then explain its meaning and the context in which it has developed. For the three misquoted items give the correct phrase and then its meaning and context.

	Word or phrase	Is it correct? If not, what should it be?	Meaning and context
1	Twigloo		
2	Clear green water		
3	Decaf		
4	Set aside		
5	Wicked		
6	Rail rage		
7	Serial killer		
8	Mule		
9	Attitude		

THE FULL MONTY

	Word or phrase	Is it correct? If not, what should it be?	Meaning and context
10	Tree hugger		
11	Sound bite		
12	Three-strikes		
13	Racket abuse		
14	Mosh		
15	Wannabe		
16	Hacker		
17	Lion economies		
18	Stonking		
19	Mouse potato		
20	Bail bandit		

THE FULL MONTY

Teaching notes

The development of language is a key theme for all teachers, but especially those of English. One of the exciting features of language for children who love words is that it is organic - it moves, it changes, it adds new words, others fall into disuse or go out of fashion.

The Full Monty takes its title from a phrase that now has a dramatic new meaning as a result of the record-breaking film of the same name. Telling the children that they are now going to do *The Full Monty* often produces a very amused response and how we need enjoyment in the classroom!

There follow, on two separate sheets, 'solutions' to the words and phrases in the exercise. These are only suggested meanings and contexts. The ways in which meanings are expressed can vary considerably while still explaining the essential points. Indeed, comparison of differing answers would be a valuable activity in itself. The contexts and groupings suggested are also quite arbitrary. A number of appropriate alternatives are equally valid. Classification is a higher-order thinking skill that is important in its own right.

Contexts

This work can be undertaken in a number of ways:

❖ as classwork for individuals

❖ as classwork for pairs or small groups

❖ as differentiated homework for able pupils

❖ as a discussion piece

❖ as a team activity in a set, but relatively short, time. 'Working against the clock' injects pace and urgency and operating in this way is a good foil to other activities where reflection and a longer time span are desirable.

Further work

1   Pupils could explore the process by which new words and phrases enter into the language.

2   The notion of particular people, such as those representing the '*Oxford Dictionary of New Words*', giving the 'official stamp of approval' to new words would be an interesting point to discuss.

3   Where words are not new but rather their meaning has changed, there are humorous possibilities in exploring the misconceptions that can take place between different generations.

4   Pupils could seek out further examples beyond the twenty used here, perhaps defining the meaning and the context as before.

THE FULL MONTY

Solutions

	Word or phrase	Is it correct? If not, what should it be?	Meaning and context
1	Twigloo	CORRECT	Form of temporary shelter made of branches and used especially by environmental protestors. Twig + igloo. ENVIRONMENT
2	Clear green water	MISQUOTED Should be: Clear blue water	Ideological gap between the two main UK political parties. Blue is also associated with Conservatives. Used by Michael Portillo. POLITICAL
3	Decaf	CORRECT	Decaffeinated coffee. More and more popular recently - worries about ill effects of caffeine. LIFESTYLE/HEALTH
4	Set aside	CORRECT	Farmland taken out of use to reduce the production of unwanted crops. Subsidies are paid. BUSINESS
5	Wicked	CORRECT	New use - great, wonderful: reversal of meaning. POPULAR CULTURE
6	Rail rage	MISQUOTED Should be: Road rage	Aggressive behaviour by drivers. MODERN SOCIETY
7	Serial killer	CORRECT	A murderer who carries out a number of killings, sometimes for reasons peculiar to them. MODERN SOCIETY
8	Mule	CORRECT	New use - carrier of illegal drugs. Always meant a carrier - perhaps also implies 'stupidity'. MODERN SOCIETY
9	Attitude	CORRECT	New use - very independent, perhaps arrogant, highly individual. Can indicate difficult. LIFESTYLE
10	Tree hugger	CORRECT	Mocking term for an environmental protester. Literal and symbolic. ENVIRONMENT
11	Sound bite	CORRECT	Short, dramatic piece in a speech etc. to produce maximum effect; or a one-liner. POLITICS

Effective Resources for Able and Talented Children © Barry Teare (Network Educational Press, 1999)

THE FULL MONTY

Solutions

	Word or phrase	Is it correct? If not, what should it be?	Meaning and context
12	Three-strikes	CORRECT	From baseball, three attempted hits and out. In USA, three serious convictions lead to mandatory life sentence. Can refer to more general behaviour. PEOPLE
13	Racket abuse	CORRECT	Wrongful use - in tennis hitting net or an object, throwing down the racket in temper. SPORT
14	Mosh	CORRECT	To dance wildly, jumping, crashing into others. Could come from 'mash'. POPULAR CULTURE
15	Wannabe	CORRECT	One who wishes to emulate someone else - aspiring, inspired by envy. From 'want to be'. POPULAR CULTURE
16	Hacker	CORRECT	Computer enthusiast, normally applied to one gaining unauthorised access to computer files. From verb 'hack'. COMPUTERS
17	Lion economies	MISQUOTED Should be: Tiger economies	The more successful economies of areas such as Singapore, South Korea (until 1998!). Tiger - fierce, energetic. BUSINESS
18	Stonking	CORRECT	Slang - very impressive, exciting. From noun 'stonk' - a military bombardment. POPULAR CULTURE
19	Mouse potato	CORRECT	Slang - someone who spends a lot of time in front of a computer. From 'couch potato'. POPULAR CULTURE
20	Bail bandit	CORRECT	A person who commits one or more extra crimes while on bail. A growing concern. PEOPLE

NOTE: THE CONTEXT CLASSIFICATIONS ARE SUGGESTIONS ONLY. OTHER GROUPINGS MAY BE EQUALLY VALID. THIS COULD LEAD TO INTERESTING DISCUSSION WORK.

POETIC LICENCE

Poetic licence is a literary term meaning that you are allowed some freedom or latitude to complete your work.

Your task

Go and find practical examples of the fifteen literary terms below. You may need to take advantage of poetic licence!

1   onomatopoeia

Meaning   _____

Example   _____

Explanation   _____

2   alliteration

Meaning   _____

Example   _____

Explanation   _____

3   palindrome

Meaning   _____

Example   _____

Explanation   _____

4   pathetic fallacy

Meaning   _____

Example   _____

Explanation   _____

5   euphemism

Meaning   _____

Example   _____

Explanation   _____

6   transferred epithet

Meaning   _____

Example   _____

Explanation   _____

7   metaphor

Meaning   _____

Example   _____

Explanation   _____

POETIC LICENCE

8 riddle

Meaning _____

Example _____

Explanation _____

9 simile

Meaning _____

Example _____

Explanation _____

10 proverb

Meaning _____

Example _____

Explanation _____

11 symbol

Meaning _____

Example _____

Explanation _____

12 hyperbole

Meaning _____

Example _____

Explanation _____

13 antonomasia

Meaning _____

Example _____

Explanation _____

14 homograph

Meaning _____

Example _____

Explanation _____

15 idiom

Meaning _____

Example _____

Explanation _____

POETIC LICENCE

Teaching notes

Literary terms in a list, or in books such as the splendid *'Oxford Concise Dictionary of Literary Terms'* by Chris Baldick (Oxford University Press, 1990), may not stir the excitement at first glance. However, they are valuable tools in enhancing our own vocabulary and language usage, and also in the criticism and discussion of texts. To the lover of words some of their names are intriguing - 'transferred epithet' and 'antonomasia'. For many other children, they can be brought to life through imaginative delivery.

The *Poetic Licence* worksheet instructs pupils to find practical examples of the fifteen literary terms listed. Two approaches are suggested here.

1 Pupils could use picture books and storybooks. To make alternative use of such books for younger children, pupils can be asked to use them to find examples of the literary terms. For example, a picture book called *'Old Farm, New Farm'* can be used to illustrate pathetic fallacy. Books by John Burningham, Raymond Briggs, Quentin Blake and Colin Thompson should also prove to be rich in examples.

2 Pupils could look around the site or around home to spot practical examples. This approach has its limitations in that it depends upon the age, and therefore the independence, of the children involved. However, it can produce some very imaginative and creative observation and thinking.

Effective Resources for Able and Talented Children © Barry Teare (Network Educational Press, 1999)

POETIC LICENCE

The fifteen terms

Onomatopoeia	Words that imitate the sound they make e.g. buzz
Alliteration	Initial letters repeated e.g. crouching, cautious cat
Palindrome	A word that is the same forwards and backwards e.g. deed
Pathetic fallacy	Natural phenomena behave as humans or fit with your mood e.g. a miserable grey day
Euphemism	A mild or indirect reference e.g. light-fingered, for a thief
Transferred epithet	An adjective is transferred from one noun to another by association e.g. sick room, when it is the people who are sick
Metaphor	A description that is imaginatively, not literally, applicable e.g. a glaring error
Riddle	A puzzling description to challenge the reader to identify it e.g. What is put on the table, cut, but never eaten? A pack of cards
Simile	A comparison of one thing with another of a different kind e.g. as useful as a chocolate teapot
Proverb	A short saying expressing some general truth or suspicion e.g. enough is as good as a feast
Symbol	Something that stands for or represents something else e.g. green for envy
Hyperbole	A deliberate exaggeration used for effect e.g. 'How many millions of times have I told you?'
Antonomasia	A proper name is replaced with an adjective, official address or other indirect description: includes using a famous person's name to convey a suggested shared quality e.g. a Goliath
Homograph	Words that are spelled the same way but have different meanings e.g. order, means instruction or command, religious group, peaceful condition, sequence
Idiom	A saying whose meaning is not the same as that of its component parts e.g. raining cats and dogs

Effective Resources for Able and Talented Children © Barry Teare (Network Educational Press, 1999)

Theme Two: *Language Across the Curriculum*

Some years ago it was fashionable to have a whole-school policy on language across the curriculum. Many principles and practices on spelling, vocabulary and a host of other issues were included in such a policy so that all members of staff could work together.

The focus of this theme is somewhat different. It concerns the development and encouragement of specialist language within curriculum areas. This area has been the subject of criticism in reports over a period of time, following observations that pupils do not use specialist language sufficiently. Indeed, the problem has been a contributory factor leading to the establishment of numeracy projects.

Most sections of the National Curriculum refer to specialist vocabulary. The Scottish 5-14 Guidelines, too, state frequently that:

> *...all pupils should be encouraged to learn, understand, and use the language, terminology and symbols appropriate to the area of study.*

Labelling diagrams, naming equipment, communicating ideas and so on all require the development of specialist language. It has other very important purposes too, such as to facilitate thinking and to encourage understanding of the essential qualities of concepts within specific and succinct vocabulary. To define something exactly is much more than a matter of words - it also demonstrates clear understanding of key concepts.

DEPICT (page 67) is very much involved with the language of concepts as well as word play and visual representation, which is a preferred outcome for some children. Two specific examples are included - one historical, one geographical. Concepts from any area of the curriculum could be treated in a similar way.

Quintessential Qualities (page 71) combines the specialist language initially of science, history and geography with word play in the form of alliteration. This can be applied to other subjects. Understanding of key concepts is at the heart of the tasks.

Four (page 73) is a combination of English language and mathematical language with some cryptic clues included as well. Pupils can then work on a number of their own choice.

The examples given here represent only the 'tip of the iceberg'. Anything that causes interest, produces a challenge, and is enjoyable while encouraging practice of specialist language, which in turn enhances understanding, is worth including. It is worth noting that CASE (Cognitive Acceleration through Science Education) has a strong language component at the start of sections of work. You could, of course, take a television game such as 'Call My Bluff' but play it within a subject area such as science, geography, mathematics, philosophy and so on. Pupils preparing the material for such an exercise would be as valuable as playing the game itself.

Another route to developing language across the curriculum in this way is to increase the availability of subject-specific dictionaries in the classroom. It is more effective to provide a mathematics dictionary or a geography dictionary when working in these areas, for example, than to expect children to plough through a more general dictionary.

In Theme Five: **Numeracy, Mathematics** there are pieces of work that involve much mathematical language, especially *Acute* (page 105), *A Calculated Risk* (page 108) and *Board with Numbers?* (page 113). Language is also a key element of *Professor Malaprop* (page 129) in Theme Six: **Science**.

Effective Resources for Able and Talented Children © Barry Teare (Network Educational Press, 1999)

DATA
EPIGRAMS
PHRASES
IMAGES
CONCEPTS
THOUGHTS

DEPICT

Example 1

kingdom

'We'

ELIZABETH

HENRY

| Monarch of all he/she surveys |

hereditary

royal assent   coronation

constitutional

| Queen bee |

WINDSOR   figurehead

| King for a day |

cavaliers   despot

| King of the castle |

divine right   **MONARCHY**   sovereign

| To Queen it | line of succession

CHARLES

queen's English

royalist

BALMORAL

DEPICT

Example 2

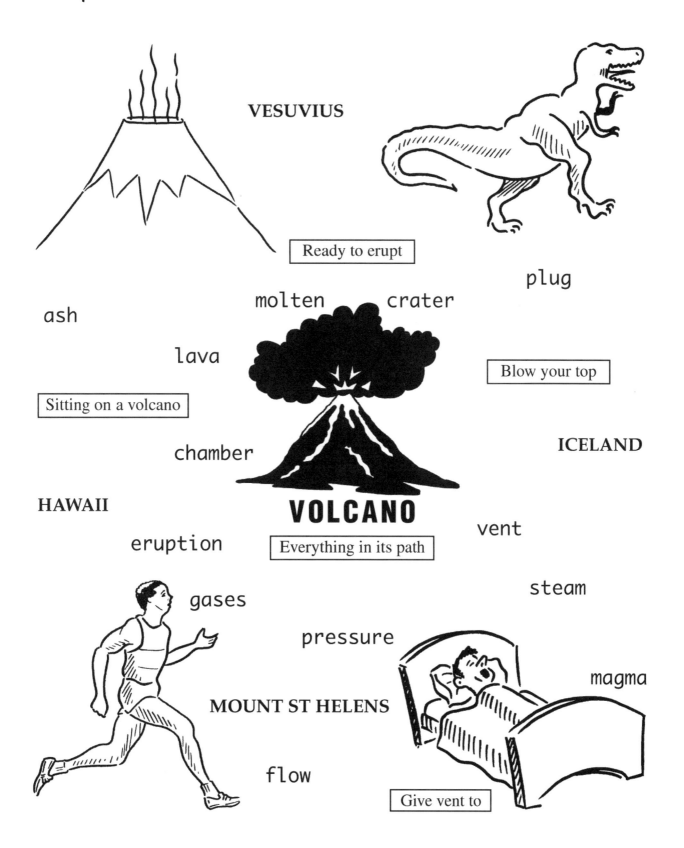

VESUVIUS

Ready to erupt

plug

ash

molten   crater

lava

Blow your top

Sitting on a volcano

chamber

ICELAND

HAWAII

VOLCANO

Everything in its path

vent

eruption

steam

gases

pressure

magma

MOUNT ST HELENS

flow

Give vent to

DEPICT

Introduction

The word 'DEPICT' has been used as an acronym for Data, Epigrams, Phrases, Images, Concepts and Thoughts (page 67). Following a discussion about the nature and aims of this exercise, pupils could be asked to produce either a totally different acronym that explains it, or a set of different words to fit the existing title. This would be a worthwhile activity given that this piece of work is very much about word play as well as different representations of concepts.

Teaching notes

In this exercise, pupils are encouraged to develop their understanding of concepts, and practise using specific and appropriate language by putting together words and phrases that are closely associated with a main concept, with pictures of linked ideas and some common sayings. The two examples provided are based around the words 'Monarchy' and 'Volcano'. Pupils could work first with these two sheets to understand the principles behind them and to make suggestions as to meaning and interpretation.

The teacher and/or pupils could then select new concept words, from history, geography or any other curriculum area, and a set of similar sheets could be produced, to include the following features:

❖ selection of associated words and phrases within a finite space, which encourages understanding of the concept and the identification of what are considered 'the essential ingredients'
❖ pictures illustrating ideas linked with the main concept, which allow a different form of representation for those who favour visual inputs and outputs
❖ common sayings associated with the main concept, which allow word play, and in turn enliven pupils' vocabulary for reading, writing and speaking

For the record, the two given examples were designed to include the following points.

Monarchy
❖ some famous kings and queens and their residences
❖ some variations on associated concepts such as 'constitutional', 'despot', 'figurehead', 'hereditary'
❖ an idea of the privileged and commanding position of the monarchy, expressed in well known sayings
❖ a chess piece to represent a king, a lion for 'King of the Beasts' and a stag for 'Monarch of the Glen'

Volcano
❖ names of some famous examples and locations of volcanoes
❖ vocabulary associated with volcanoes, which illustrates knowledge and understanding of the component parts
❖ an idea of the explosive nature and power of volcanoes, as suggested by common sayings such as 'blow your top' and 'everything in its path'
❖ pictures of a dinosaur, a bed and a runner to illustrate the concepts of extinct, dormant and active

Effective Resources for Able and Talented Children © Barry Teare (Network Educational Press, 1999)

QUINTESSENTIAL QUALITIES

Scintillating Science Speak

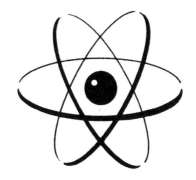

Bacteria: breakdown, bountiful, breeding
Starch: saccharide, stored, sustaining

Hearing Heady History

Reform: redressing, rectifying, reassessing, radical
Empire: expansion, empress/emperor, extensive, exploiting/enlightening
Crusade: Christian, campaigning, conviction, converting

GENERATING GEOGRAPHICAL GLOSSARY

Tundra: treeless, tremble, tough
Earthquake: epicentre, energy, earthshaking, endemic

Your tasks

- Explain the rationale behind the title *Quintessential Qualities*.
- Add examples of your own in the subject areas given above.
- Choose other subject areas, give them a suitable title and construct examples.

QUINTESSENTIAL QUALITIES

Teaching notes

This set of suggestions is to encourage pupils to use subject-specific language and to develop understanding of key concepts while enjoying one particular form of word play.

Alliteration has been used for the overall title, for the sub-titles relating to science, history and geography, and for the words relating to knowledge and concepts. For any chosen curriculum area there is an element of English via word play and vocabulary extension.

The rationale behind the overall title *Quintessential Qualities* involves:

❖ use of the term 'quintessential qualities' to indicate that pupils should be concentrating upon key features in explaining a phenomenon or concept

❖ a lead example of alliteration

The three sub-titles again use alliteration, but they also convey a meaning about each subject's vocabulary. Terms associated with each subject are followed by a small group of words that have the same initial letter as the lead word and which help to convey some of the essential elements associated with that lead word. Thus, in the science section, 'bacteria' break down organic material, exist in tremendous volume and multiply rapidly. Under the history heading, 'exploiting/enlightening' suggest alternative views of the value of 'empire'. One of the geography examples, 'earthquake', has an associated word, 'endemic', to convey the uneven worldwide distribution of earthquake activity.

Pupils are requested to find other examples in the three given subject areas. Then there is the opportunity to move into other curriculum areas, which necessitates the creation of a suitable alliterative title. Children would be assisted in these further examples by the availability of subject-specific dictionaries.

Key elements

The initial study, together with further work, serves the following purposes:

❖ word play, especially alliteration
❖ vocabulary extension
❖ practice in the key thinking skills of application and analysis
❖ response at an individual level, thus involving differentiation by outcome
❖ use of specialist dictionaries
❖ understanding and demonstration of key concepts and ideas

Contexts

The exercise could also possibly be used:

❖ as differentiated homework
❖ as the basis for a class discussion
❖ as extension material for the more able
❖ during an enrichment session
❖ as a competition
❖ as part of a class topic, in written form

Effective Resources for Able and Talented Children © Barry Teare (Network Educational Press, 1999)

FOUR

Your task

Explain how each of the following involves the number four or the word four.

1   time
2   April
3   quadruped
4   slang for a blow with the fist
5   preparing for a game of bridge
6   'freedom' of the United States of America
7   a sporting boundary
8   quadruple
9   autumn, spring, etc.
10 the Press
11 calling birds
12 a navigable course on television
13 the internal combustion engine
14 earth, air, etc.
15 'notice' of a Sherlock Holmes story
16 quadrennial
17 old-fashioned sleeping accommodation
18 'serious' sound broadcasting
19 blood, phlegm, etc.
20 quadrilateral
21 North, South, etc.
22 quadrant
23 diamonds, hearts, etc.
24 a lucky plant formation
25 the Gospels

FOUR

Solution

1   the fourth dimension

2   the fourth month of the year

3   an animal with four legs

4   'a fourpenny one'

5   making up a four to play

6   July 4th - Independence Day

7   scoring a four at cricket

8   to multiply by four

9   the four seasons

10   known as the 'Fourth Estate'

11   the present on the fourth day of Christmas

12   Channel 4

13   four-stroke engine

14   the four elements

15   *'The Sign of Four'*

16   occurring every four years

17   four-poster bed

18   Radio 4

19   the four humours of the body

20   having four sides

21   the four cardinal points of the compass

22   one of the four equal parts of the circumference of a circle

23   the four suits in a pack of cards

24   a four-leaf clover

25   the first four books of the New Testament

Effective Resources for Able and Talented Children © Barry Teare (Network Educational Press, 1999)

Theme Three: *Reading*

What should able children be encouraged to read? We may actually be asking two questions here:

❖ What should able readers read?

❖ How should able children, who don't like reading, be encouraged to read?

The second question may well involve in its response a much wider view of suitable material than fiction, and it will probably be more pertinent to boys than to girls. Those concerned with boys' underachievement, including that of able boys, have suggested a range of strategies to encourage reading, including greater use of non-fiction, inclusion of more male role models, use of magazines on subjects such as computers rather than conventional books and a search for more 'boy-orientated' content within novels.

Advising able readers is an interesting area. Followers of Roald Dahl will remember Matilda, who asked the librarian for help when she claimed that she had read all the children's books. At the tender age of four years and three months, Matilda was recommended 'Great Expectations' and after the successful and enjoyable completion of Dickens' masterpiece, she was encouraged to work her way through a weighty list of 'classics'.

What would you advise, and on what grounds? With the current wealth of new children's books there is not the necessity to tackle Matilda's list. Many companies such as Puffin, Waterstones and Dillons, produce very informative and helpful parents' guides. Some use the phrase 'fluent readers', but the Puffin guide actually refers to 'gifted readers'. Jenny Green, of that company, has produced a splendid catalogue called 'Stretching the Gifted Reader', which discusses principles behind recommendations, identifies key categories and then lists individual books. She has written an excellent article for the National Association for Able Children in Education (NACE) on the same theme. It is certainly worthwhile to give some thought to this issue.

The National Curriculum gives assistance to teachers regarding the key skills for reading at Key Stage 2:

> *They should be encouraged to respond imaginatively to the plot, characters, ideas and vocabulary and organisation of language in literature. They should be taught to use inference and deduction.*

Similarly, the English Language section of the Scottish 5-14 Guidelines suggests that children should be encouraged to read:

> *... to gain imaginative and aesthetic pleasure.*

The study of genre is promoted strongly in the Scottish 5-14 Guidelines. The wonderful phrase 'imaginative versatility' is used in relation to pupils beyond Level E.

Within the structure of the Literacy Hour there is shared text work, which is a balance of reading and writing. As the teacher supports the reading, it is intended that texts can be chosen that are beyond the independent reading levels of some members of the class. This 'selecting upwards' is a positive point for able children but the texts used need to be able to satisfy their needs. These needs are likely to be based not only on greater technical ability but also on their appreciation of different levels of meaning and more sophisticated characterisation, of word humour and of the absurd, and on their greater maturity in exploring the issues within the book. The quality of questioning by the teacher is vital if able pupils' needs are to be met.

In the Literacy Hour, there is also a twenty-minute period of group and independent work that includes reading. Ability grouping seems inevitable. Here it is hoped that more able children will extend themselves but the guided programme is important if that is to be achieved. The opportunities need to be exploited to the full.

In the following exercises, *Mole, Rat, Badger, Toad and ... Who?* (page 77) provides a number of opportunities for imaginative exploration of text by making changes to characters, sequencing or plots. It is open-ended, allowing individual responses. There is the clear possibility of humorous development. The key area of hypothesising is a strong element. It fits calls to respond imaginatively and to use imaginative versatility in the guidelines quoted above. Particular books are used as stimuli but pupils can range over a wider selection of their own choice.

The Bare Bones (page 81) looks at the creation of stories. It involves making connections between given items, and able children make much of such opportunities. Genre is a feature. The suggested method of outcome is a verbal presentation from a team, which fits guidelines on speaking and gives some children a preferred outcome.

Tangled Tales (page 84) encourages wider knowledge of children's literature through a light-hearted piece, which can assist listening skills and be extended into a piece of writing demanding particular abilities.

One of the pieces of work in Theme Seven: **Logical Thought**, *According to the Book* (page 155), centres around descriptions of twenty very good novels for children, and also terms associated with books, thus fitting the vocabulary sections of reading guidelines in both Scotland and England.

The commercially produced resources list in Section Two of this book contains recommendations for a small number of recent novels plus details of guides and 'Young Book Trust' materials.

MOLE, RAT, BADGER, TOAD AND ... WHO?

Adding a character

📖 Kenneth Grahame, *'The Wind in the Willows'*

Imagine that you could add an extra creature as a major character in *'The Wind in the Willows'*.

1 Which creature would it be?
2 Why?
3 How would it change the story?

Timeswitch books

📖 Terry Pratchett, *'Johnny and the Bomb'*
📖 Melvin Burgess, *'An Angel for May'*

In Terry Pratchett's book, Johnny Maxwell and his friends are involved in a timeswitch between the present day and the Second World War. Melvin Burgess' main character, Tam, is involved in a similar time slip in *'An Angel for May'*.

Choose one of these two books.

1 Change the period involved in the timeswitch.
2 Say what made you choose that particular period.
3 Indicate some of the consequences of your change to the course of the book.

Changing roles

📖 Mark Twain, *'The Prince and the Pauper'*

Some famous stories, such as *'The Prince and the Pauper'*, centre on the adventures of two people who exchange roles in life.

1 Can you quote other books where this happens?
2 Make your own suggestions as to exchanges of role that would make for interesting reading.

MOLE, RAT, BADGER, TOAD AND ... WHO?

A geographical switch

Theresa Tomlinson, *'Meet Me by the Steelmen'*

This wonderful book is centred on Sheffield. It has a range of interesting features, one of which is the history of the steel industry and the people employed in that industry.

1   Name other books where the location is critical to the development of the plot.
2   Choose a different location for Theresa Tomlinson's story, and speculate upon the changes that would need to occur in the book.

The vanishing character

1   Choose a book that you know well and decide upon the removal of a key character.
2   Explain how you would change the story to accommodate the disappearance of this person.

A detective story

Malorie Blackman, *'Lie Detectives'*

Choose a detective-type story, such as *'Lie Detectives'*.

1   Write down the key points in the solution of the mystery or crime.
2   Take the story back one hundred years and find historically-correct alternatives to the detective methods used.

MOLE, RAT, BADGER, TOAD AND ... WHO?

'Political correction'

📖 Enid Blyton, *'The Secret Seven'* and *'The Famous Five'* books

Enid Blyton is an incredibly popular children's author. Her books have sold in enormous numbers. She has written many series but two of the best known are those that involve The Secret Seven and The Famous Five. Enid Blyton has been much criticised. One reason is that her characters tend to be gender-stereotypes, and the roles of girls are often reduced. In fact, one book of criticism on gender roles in children's literature was actually called *'Pour Out the Cocoa, Janet'*, referring to a character in The Secret Seven books.

1   Choose a story involving The Secret Seven or The Famous Five in which you believe such gender-stereotyping takes place, quoting examples.
2   Write a short plan for a 'politically correct' version of the same book.
3   Comment upon whether you think that the changes improve the book or otherwise.

Prequels

1   Take a story that you know well, which does not quite 'begin at the beginning', explaining why this is so.
2   Write an outline for a 'prequel' that would lead satisfactorily into the book you have chosen.

Sequels

1   Take a story that you know well, which you believe has left scope for further development, explaining why this is so.
2   Write an outline for a 'sequel' that would take the story on satisfactorily.

Alternative work

Some of the activities above centre upon a particular book, which you may not know. In those cases, you can apply the same techniques to a book that you do know well.

Alternatively, you may wish to suggest other ways in which books could be changed creatively.

MOLE, RAT, BADGER, TOAD AND ... WHO?

Teaching notes

Imaginative response to text is very much encouraged in the National Curriculum and Scottish 5-14 Guidelines, and it is strongly implied in the Literacy Framework. The type of activity suggested here will involve a number of important thinking skills:

❖ analysis of what has to be done and within what context

❖ application of an idea or principle to other examples

❖ evaluation of devices and methods

❖ synthesis - pulling information together and making something new of it

❖ hypothesising on the likely outcomes of changes and switches

❖ imaginative and creative thinking via alternatives

In addition, the activity is likely to lead to a number of beneficial outcomes. Many able children have a particular style of humour, which can be a strong feature in this work. One child's response to 'The Wind in the Willows' was to suggest that Mr Toad, senior, might still be around to influence his son for good or for ill. Familiarity with techniques such as timeswitch and role exchange can be increased. Children can be encouraged to develop an understanding of style and author-intent, through prequels and sequels. Issues such as gender can be explored through the different approaches taken by authors.

Certain books are used, which provide suitable contexts for the ideas. Children are, however, encouraged to apply the same ideas to other texts with which they might be more familiar. Teacher guidance in this matter might be of value. Otherwise guidance should be kept to a minimum. As long as children know that the 'doors and windows are open' and they can fly off in all sorts of directions, lively, imaginative and individual responses are likely.

Contexts

This piece of work could be used in a variety of ways:

❖ during an enrichment session

❖ as a feature of a Book Week

❖ as a basis for written work in the normal classroom situation

❖ to suggest an issue as the subject of a debate

❖ as a basis for general discussion

❖ within the guided and independent work section of the Literacy Hour

❖ for differentiated homework

❖ as an activity for a school Book Club

❖ in conjunction with a visiting writer or poet

Effective Resources for Able and Talented Children © Barry Teare (Network Educational Press, 1999)

THE BARE BONES

Manuscript number

Writing team

Descriptions of items

Outline plan

EXACT SETTING

GENRE

TITLE

FURTHER RESEARCH

THE BASIC STORYLINE
(Use the set items for the manuscript. Please continue over the page.)

THE BARE BONES

Teaching notes

In this piece of work children plan the 'bare bones' of a story, using a good deal of open-endedness but also making connections from given points. Indeed, there is a theory that the imposition of some parameters can sometimes enhance creativity. The consideration of genre is an integral part of the piece, which is of course a major theme in guidelines in both England and Scotland.

The Bare Bones is best carried out as a team activity, and the plan preferably written within a fixed time-scale. The teacher must provide certain physical items:

❖ pages from an old motorists' map book showing different types of locations (urban, rural, 'out in the wilds', coastal)

❖ miscellaneous artefacts such as bits of jewellery, stones, coins, railway timetables, business cards, etc.

❖ photographs of adults, children and animals - either singly or in groups (these can be taken from magazines etc.)

Each team is given:

❖ one map page

❖ two artefacts

❖ five photographs, mixed in terms of subject (e.g. type of animal, ages of people, number of characters)

Pupils' work

Each team discusses the items, which are provided in a numbered manuscript bag (this can just be a large brown envelope). Within the time limit (perhaps 40 minutes) the team creates 'the bare bones' of a story that is located somewhere within the area shown on the map page. They describe the two artefacts or items on the pupil sheet, and these two items have to play a part in the story. From the five photographs, the group has to use at least three to provide the main characters for the story. If a photograph is used all the people on it must be included.

A genre is selected and indicated on the sheet. The main part of the work is to put together the outline of the plot but within the limitations of the location, the items, the people and the chosen genre. As this only constitutes 'the bare bones' or starting point, there is a section on the pupil sheet to record what further research the group think would be necessary for the development of the story.

Outcome

After discussion within each team, the sheet is filled in.

Manuscript number:	indicated on the bag or envelope
Writing team:	the names of the children in the group
Descriptions of items:	the two artefacts or items provided
Exact setting:	a location taken from the map page provided
Genre:	detective, romance, historical, etc.

Effective Resources for Able and Talented Children © Barry Teare (Network Educational Press, 1999)

Title:	a suitable title for the plot and genre
Further research:	what else the team would do in writing the book, depending upon the particular story, to provide authenticity and to continue the story
The basic storyline:	a reasonable outline to give a real feel for what is to happen, including, of course, the items and the people from the photographs

The exercise can be taken a step further by asking one or more members from each team to give a short verbal presentation to the class based upon the discussion and the pupil sheet.

Feedback
The teacher or another adult, or indeed another child, should provide feedback on the strengths and weaknesses of each presentation.

The criteria are likely to include:
- ❖ the skill with which the items, location and people have been woven into the story so that they fit naturally together
- ❖ the appropriateness and sophistication of the title
- ❖ the quality of the basic storyline
- ❖ the co-operation between members of the team
- ❖ the quality of the verbal presentation
- ❖ the thinking behind the suggestions for further research

This exercise can be used in a competitive situation if the teacher wishes, but there is no need to go that route. What matters is that there is quality feedback.

Key elements
- ❖ open-endedness
- ❖ collaborative discussion
- ❖ verbal outcome
- ❖ imagination and creativity
- ❖ understanding of the planning for a book
- ❖ analysis of what needs to be done
- ❖ synthesis - pulling the parts together and making something new and personal from them
- ❖ meeting a deadline
- ❖ understanding of genre
- ❖ use of text techniques
- ❖ immediate feedback
- ❖ opportunity to evaluate the work of other teams

Variations
A particular pattern has been described here in some detail with the aim of helping the teacher as much as possible. These guidelines are just that - they are not designed to be prescriptive. The same basic exercise could be carried out in a variety of ways if the teacher so prefers. This could be an individual piece of work, perhaps a piece of homework. It could be attempted in pairs. There does not have to be a verbal presentation when the pupil sheet has been completed.

TANGLED TALES

Passage one

It was a dark and stormy night. The trees moved back and forward casting eerie shapes on the ground. The night watchmen thought that they were going to earn their money the hard way. They had been employed to look after the site of a proposed new road on the edge of a great forest. To the south was a river and the men could hear the wind in the willows.

Some of the men were concerned that they might become the targets of conservationists who were protesting about the development. This was not true of Clint who feared nothing. He was known as the iron man by the rest of the team. Clint saw the supervisor, Thomas Jones, leaving the site for home. 'Goodnight, Mister Tom!' Clint shouted and he was acknowledged by a wave from his boss. 'I'm glad I'm off home,' said Tom. 'Anyway you five have a wonderful time,' he said sarcastically.

Clint went back to the others. They were arguing about the rights and wrongs of the development they had been hired to protect. David was not sure that he was in the right job. He supported the return of the wolf to the area. David loved the outdoors. At home he also looked for the midnight fox on its nightly excursion for food. He thought back to a previous contract in the wilds where on some nights he would glance skywards hoping for a sight of the Northern Lights. He was jolted out of his mind wanderings by raised voices. 'Who says animals don't have rights?' one of the gang was saying. One of the men, who had no sympathy with environmental arguments, shouted the first man down. 'I'm tired of all this "only you can save mankind" stuff,' he mocked. 'You people live in a world of your own. You are unreal.' Only Bob was not involved in the argument. He was busy munching an early supper as usual. The rest of the men called him Mr Greedy.

David shrugged his shoulders and moved away from the noise. He heard a bird singing its heart out. 'Why don't they shut up and listen to the nightingale?' he thought. (14)

TANGLED TALES

Passage two

Roger stood shivering near the red wall, waiting for his friends to arrive. Although it was the twelfth day of July, the weather was unseasonably cold and Roger wished that he had worn something warmer. He put his hand onto the wall. It felt stone cold. There was a terrific noise to the west and a flash lit up the sky. A storm was on its way. We might as well be in the grip of winter, thought Roger, noting the thunder and lightnings.

'Boo!' said a voice close to him. Roger jumped in fright. His friend Susan emerged from the shadows. 'Where's Wally?' she asked. 'He was off school today ill,' replied Roger. 'Perhaps he needs some of George's marvellous medicine,' responded Susan.

They waited a few minutes more, getting more and more impatient. Then, across the road, they spotted another of their friends. 'Here comes Charlie Moon,' said Susan, pleased for a break in the boredom. With Charlie was a tiny Yorkshire terrier. 'I've never seen a dog so small,' laughed Peter. Charlie was none too pleased about Peter's attitude. 'I'm sorry,' said Peter, 'but he's hardly the hound of the Baskervilles.'

The three children with the tiny dog chattered together waiting for the late arrivals. A boy they did not know came up to them. 'Wally said you would be here. He can't come out tonight. I am David, his cousin. I hope you don't mind if I tag along with you.' 'No that's fine,' said Susan. 'We are waiting for Matilda but she is very late.' 'Perhaps she has been kidnapped,' joked Peter. Then his face clouded over. 'A more likely reason is that she has had problems with the bully who lives near her.' The children went silent thinking about the problems that their friend faced from the unpleasant girl who bragged that her nickname was 'otherwise known as Sheila The Great'.

'That girl is going to get into a lot of trouble,' commented Susan. 'Not only is she unpleasant to anyone she regards as weak but she is flouting rules about the computer network at school. If any of the teachers discover that she is a hacker she will be up before Mr Grimsby.' 'Yes, the demon headmaster,' smirked Peter, but he wasn't laughing inside. Visiting room 13, 'unlucky for some', was how the pupils described a trip to see the headteacher. Unfortunately, justice was not always done and the guilty party was not punished on every occasion. (20)

TANGLED TALES

Teaching notes

Two passages are provided, which have been written to be as natural and flowing as possible while at the same time fitting in a number of children's book titles: 'Passage one' contains fourteen titles and 'Passage two', includes twenty. These and the authors are listed on the following page. It is possible that, inadvertently, other titles have been included, which children might identify. These answers will have to be judged individually, and preferably following some substantiation from the child.

There are different ways of using the two passages.

A verbal delivery

The teacher could read a passage out, having warned the class to try to spot the titles. It is fair to say how many titles there are in each passage. Reading out the passage only once clearly makes the task more difficult than with a repeat. The children can work individually, in pairs or in teams. If the third option is used the teams need a short time to compare their thoughts and come to a joint conclusion.

This approach encourages listening skills. Careful attention is needed to spot the less obvious examples such as 'Unreal'.

A reading delivery

In this version, the passages should be given out to the class to read. The aim is exactly the same and again the work can be done individually, in pairs or in teams or groups. This method reduces the difficulty, as being able to re-read the passage again and again makes the task easier than spotting the titles while listening to the passages being read out.

A written extension

For able pupils whose writing flows and who are sophisticated in their choice of vocabulary and constructions, there is an obvious extension. Having familiarised themselves with the process, the children could be asked to write passages of their own based on the same principles. The criteria for assessing the children's passages are likely to be:

❖ the number of titles included in a reasonable length

❖ the adeptness in fitting in titles without clumsiness

❖ the overall flow and sense maintained in the passage

There is a good opportunity here to encourage children to explore catalogues and guides in order to look for suitable titles. This exercise may itself lead to the discovery of new books and authors to read.

This is a light-hearted, fun piece but there are some obvious gains from each of the three modes. The written extension could be used in a different context such as a differentiated homework.

Effective Resources for Able and Talented Children © Barry Teare (Network Educational Press, 1999)

TANGLED TALES

Solutions

Passage one

1. *'It was a Dark and Stormy Night'*, Janet and Allan Ahlberg
2. *'The Night Watchmen'*, Helen Cresswell
3. *'The Wind in the Willows'*, Kenneth Grahame
4. *'The Iron Man'*, Ted Hughes
5. *'Goodnight, Mister Tom'*, Michelle Magorian
6. *'Five Have a Wonderful Time'*, Enid Blyton
7. *'Wolf'*, Gillian Cross
8. *'The Midnight Fox'*, Betsy Byars
9. *'Northern Lights'*, Philip Pullman
10. *'Who Says Animals Don't Have Rights?'*, Jean Ure
11. *'Only You can Save Mankind'*, Terry Pratchett
12. *'Unreal'*, Paul Jennings
13. *'Mr Greedy'*, Roger Hargreaves
14. *'Listen to the Nightingale'*, Rumer Godden

Passage two

1. *'Redwall'*, Brian Jacques
2. *'The Twelfth Day of July'*, Joan Lingard
3. *'Stone Cold'*, Robert Swindells
4. *'In the Grip of Winter'*, Colin Dann
5. *'Thunder and Lightnings'*, Jan Mark
6. *'Boo'*, Colin McNaughton
7. *'Where's Wally?'*, Martin Handford
8. *'George's Marvellous Medicine'*, Roald Dahl
9. *'Here Comes Charlie Moon'*, Shirley Hughes
10. *'A Dog So Small'*, Philippa Pearce
11. *'The Hound of the Baskervilles'*, Sir Arthur Conan-Doyle
12. *'I am David'*, Anne Holm
13. *'Matilda'*, Roald Dahl
14. *'Kidnapped'*, Robert Louis Stevenson
15. *'The Bully'*, Jan Needle
16. *'Otherwise Known As Sheila the Great'*, Judy Blume
17. *'Hacker'*, Malorie Blackman
18. *'The Demon Headmaster'*, Gillian Cross
19. *'Room 13'*, Robert Swindells
20. *'The Guilty Party'*, Joan Lingard

Theme Four: *Writing*

The greater the variety that can be used in the writing opportunities provided for children the better. The National Curriculum stresses the importance of varied purposes, an extended range of readers and using the characteristics of different kinds of writing. The Scottish 5-14 Guidelines say that:

> *...pupils will write functionally, personally and imaginatively, to convey meaning in language appropriate to audience and purpose.*

The Literacy Framework contains much advice on writing, and provides detailed instructions on a term-by-term basis. As the Literacy Hour settles down, one concern being voiced is that extended writing opportunities are difficult to organise.

As well as the general background from the curriculum documents, attention must be paid to the specific needs of more able pupils. The Scottish 5-14 Guidelines look to 'enhanced difficulty in test and task', 'increased independence of learning' and 'higher expectations of response'. They use, too, the wonderful phrase 'imaginative versatility'. Key Stage 2 of the National Curriculum states that:

> *... pupils should be taught to write in response to more demanding tasks.*

Encouraging creativity and imagination is a key feature of a curriculum for the more able and writing provides so many avenues by which to achieve this.

Consideration of what makes a task more difficult and challenging is a key factor in setting writing assignments. If pupils have to finish up with a pre-set concluding paragraph, this certainly increases the demands upon them: *And That's the End of the Story* (page 91) promotes analysis followed by imagination and creativity, but with parameters. Judgement on genre is another ingredient. This piece of work looks to individuality of response and therefore differentiation by outcome.

Straight from the Horse's Mouth (page 94) uses a variety of situations, some very serious, others humorous. It extends the range of writing tasks by taking the viewpoint of an animal and considering the different perspectives involved. Analysis of existing texts would help pupils. The outcomes can be very varied indeed. The lighter situations give a chance for able children to display the particular sense of humour that is characteristic of so many of them.

Humour plays a key role in *The Man in the Van* (page 96). The intended audience here is young readers. Analysis of Dr Seuss' methods is a necessary pre-requisite for the writing that follows. There is a particular purpose. Word humour, rhythm and zany images are powerful ingredients.

Mouthwatering (page 98) looks again at a specific purpose - that of encouraging people to eat particular dishes. It also involves a particular audience - diners of different types. Contrasting vocabulary is used to tempt people of differing palettes.

The final piece, *Opening Up a New Chapter* (page 100), is demanding and challenging in a different way to other work in this Theme. It promotes collaborative writing, which is very difficult indeed if the resulting story is to be of reasonable quality.

Writing tasks also appear in other parts of the book: *Professor Malaprop* and *Property To Let* (Theme Six: **Science**, pages 126 and 129); *According to the Evidence* (Theme Ten: **Detective Work**, page 203) and *Now You See It* (Theme Eleven: **Alternative Answers, Imagination, Creativity**, page 232).

'... AND THAT'S THE END OF THE STORY'

> ARE YOU THE SORT OF PERSON WHO TAKES A PEEK AT THE
> END OF THE BOOK BEFORE YOU REACH IT?
> WHAT IF THAT IS WHERE YOU STARTED TO THINK OF
> A STORY - AT THE END!
> HOW DIFFICULT MIGHT THAT BE?

Your task

Below are four endings to four different stories.

Choose one, or more, of the endings and then write a story that has the written paragraph as the final part. You cannot write another word after that paragraph. The contents of the paragraph will give you a number of clues as to what must be explained and described in the main part of the story. Also, give the story a suitable title.

Ending one

Susan snuggled down into the warm bed. The last few days had been incredible. She thought of the problems and difficulties that had been overcome and the near-disasters that had almost occurred. It had all finished well but it might have been a different story. Susan settled down contentedly. Perhaps the most important result was that her friendship with Anna was stronger than ever.

Ending two

Peter watched the train moving slowly away from the platform. It gathered speed, turned the corner of the line and disappeared from view. He turned away sadly, his shoulders drooping and his head bowed. Peter searched his mind. Could he have said something differently - something that would have produced a happier result?

'... AND THAT'S THE END OF THE STORY'

Ending three

The computer screen indicated that it was safe to switch off the machine. Alison did so, with trembling fingers. People said that new technology opened up new worlds but she had not expected it to be true so literally!

Ending four

The animals fell silent as the magnificent golden badger rose on its hind legs.

'Friends, we have fought a superior foe and we have triumphed against all the odds. You have shown great determination. It is only through working together that we have survived. Come, let us eat and drink, for we have certainly deserved our celebration.'

The animals followed Bachilar, their badger leader, into the glade where a wonderful feast was prepared. They were excited and happy but in all their minds were the pictures of fallen friends who would not be eating that, or any other, night.

'...AND THAT'S THE END OF THE STORY'

Teaching notes

Having some parameters can enhance creativity. In this piece of work the pupils have not got a totally free hand, but there are many different ways of reading the set endings.

The four alternatives are likely to fit different genres and thus appeal to a variety of children. The teacher might wish to decide on what length the story should be. There is also the possibility of allowing children to change the name and gender of the main character if this is considered desirable.

In all areas of the curriculum we should be looking for ways to make tasks more difficult and challenging for able pupils. In this piece of writing, using the ending to inform the story is certainly challenging especially when one considers that nothing more can be written after the designated final paragraph.

Key elements

There are key elements in the work:
- ❖ individuality of response and therefore differentiation by outcome
- ❖ analysis of the last paragraph
- ❖ imagination and creativity but within parameters
- ❖ judgement on genre and the main body of the story so that the ending is appropriate

Criteria

The quality of the work produced is likely to be judged on:
- ❖ the suitability of the title
- ❖ the degree to which the main body of the story fits the ending
- ❖ the standard of the writing
- ❖ the extent to which clues have been lifted from the ending to inform the rest of the story

STRAIGHT FROM THE HORSE'S MOUTH

> HAVE YOU EVER WONDERED WHAT IT IS LIKE TO BE A HORSE JUMPING A
> FENCE, OR A DOG SEARCHING FOR DRUGS AMONGST BAGGAGE? WHAT DOES
> THE ANIMAL THINK? WHAT IS IMPORTANT TO THE ANIMAL? HOW DIFFERENT
> IS IT TO A HUMAN VIEWPOINT?

In this activity, you are asked to write from the point of view of an animal or creature. Henrietta Branford's wonderful story *'Fire, Bed and Bone'* is told by a dog at the time of The Peasants' Revolt. *'The True Story of the Three Little Pigs'* by Jon Scieszka and Lane Smith is a very funny book in which the wolf tells the story from his own perspective.

Your tasks

- Choose one or more of the following situations.
- Work out the issues and events that would be of paramount importance to the particular animal or creature.
- Write a story, with a suitable title, from the creature's point of view.

The situations

1 a fox at the 'wrong' end of a hunt
2 a sniffer dog working at a large airport
3 an orang-utan in Indonesia watching the destruction of the forest
4 a cat living in a medieval town in England
5 a horse training for, and during, the Grand National
6 a rat at the time of the Great Plague
7 a guinea pig in a research laboratory
8 a gun dog on a shooting expedition
9 a donkey employed in beach rides for children
10 a horse at the 'Charge of the Light Brigade'
11 Dick Whittington's cat
12 a cow caught up in the BSE situation
13 the spider who frightened Little Miss Muffet
14 the cow that 'jumped over the Moon'
15 the tortoise that raced the hare in Aesop's fable

Extension work

- Make a list of situations of your own
- Choose one of them and write an appropriate story. And remember to tell it **'straight from the horse's mouth'**!

STRAIGHT FROM THE HORSE'S MOUTH

Teaching notes

Writing for different audiences and different purposes features strongly in both the National Curriculum and the Scottish 5-14 Guidelines. This unusual piece of work takes the process further.

Extracts from Henrietta Branford's excellent book *'Fire, Bed and Bone'* (Walker Books) could be used as an introduction. This would be a help to pupils to show an example of an appropriate title and to hear how the story is told. The issues and events that are important to a dog are also illustrated.

The situations have been mixed deliberately to provide different types of opportunities. Some of the examples involve serious questions about the way animals are treated in society. There are obvious links here with debates on moral and ethical issues. Some have a historical background and could be linked with work in history. Others, from nursery rhymes and other sources, have a lighter feel to them. They may well inspire a humorous account, which gives free rein to the particular sense of humour possessed by many able children.

Contexts

The work could be set in a number of contexts including:

❖ as a class activity for all, allowing differentiation by outcome

❖ as a differentiated homework

❖ as a competition with open access

❖ as an additional piece of work for children well ahead in their other activities

❖ as a task for able children during the Literacy Hour

❖ as part of an enrichment session

❖ as an activity for an extra-curricular writing club

❖ as a task for an extraction group of able writers

Extension

The extension work allows children to choose their own situations. A list in itself would be of interest, even if a full story does not follow.

THE MAN IN THE VAN

Many of us remember well the books that were used to teach us to read. Many Americans have fond memories of the Dr Seuss books. Some of the wonderful titles give a clue to the character of the books:

> *'The Cat in the Hat'*
> *'Fox in Socks'*
> *'Green Eggs and Ham'*
> *'How the Grinch Stole Christmas'*
> *'One Fish, Two Fish, Red Fish, Blue Fish'*

Can you emulate Dr Seuss?

Your tasks

- ✍ Read some of the Dr Seuss books, especially *'The Cat in the Hat'* and *'Green Eggs and Ham'.*

- ✍ Analyse the stories to determine the particular characteristics that are typical of the books.

- ✍ Write your own story entitled *'The Man in the Van'* and apply the same principles.

- ✍ If you wish, illustrate your story with appropriate drawings.

THE MAN IN THE VAN

Teaching notes

Many able children possess a particular sense of humour. They enjoy word play, double meanings, puns and word humour. The Dr Seuss books play to those features very strongly indeed.

The study of genre is an important issue in the Scottish 5-14 Guidelines on English language and in the National Curriculum. Both wish to promote a sense of appropriateness in writing:

> *...to convey meaning in language appropriate to audience and purpose.*
> Scottish 5-14 Guidelines

> *...pupils should be taught the characteristics of different kinds of writing.*
> National Curriculum

Key elements

The Man in the Van encourages a number of elements, including:

- ❖ analysis of text
- ❖ application of principles
- ❖ genre
- ❖ writing for a particular audience
- ❖ writing for a particular purpose
- ❖ word humour

Criteria

The piece of writing produced should be judged on:
- ❖ the use of the set title
- ❖ the understanding of the characteristics of Dr Seuss books - zany humour, appealing rhymes, great characters, repetition of words and sounds to help the young reader, wonderful images, short and punchy delivery, rhythm
- ❖ the application of these characteristics in their own story

The optional extra of illustrating the story will appeal to those who enjoy visual presentation.

MOUTHWATERING

When you go out for a meal, how much notice do you take of the menu? Are you tempted by the description of the dish?

Writing skills are used for a variety of purposes. A menu, skilfully written, can tempt people to dine and persuade others that their personal tastes are accommodated. This activity gives you the opportunity to do exactly these things.

Your tasks

✍ You are the owner of four different restaurants. You are trying to attract particular types of customers to each restaurant, namely:

1 those who are rather narrow and cautious in their choice of food

2 those who like to eat 'in quantity'!

3 those who are very concerned with their health and the links with food

4 those who want value for money

By very careful selection of words, phrases and sentences, explain what features of your menus would attract each of the four groups. Give each of your restaurants an appropriate name.

✍ You are Gary Gourmet, in charge of a restaurant in a four-star hotel. Your customers are likely to be impressed with appetising and colourful descriptions of the meals. For example:

CARAMELISED ORANGES DRIZZLED WITH A DRAMBUIE SAUCE

SMOKED SALMON PARCELS BURSTING WITH SUN-RIPENED TOMATOES AND PEELED PRAWNS

Write similarly appetising descriptions for dishes based upon the ingredients in this menu (you can add other ingredients within reason).

How does Gary Gourmet turn these basic ingredients into gorgeous gastronomical delights?

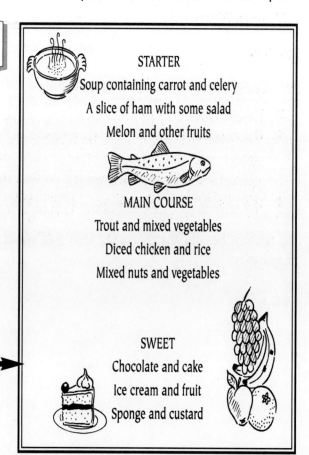

STARTER

Soup containing carrot and celery

A slice of ham with some salad

Melon and other fruits

MAIN COURSE

Trout and mixed vegetables

Diced chicken and rice

Mixed nuts and vegetables

SWEET

Chocolate and cake

Ice cream and fruit

Sponge and custard

MOUTHWATERING

Teaching notes

This activity involves a more unusual purpose for writing but one that can be powerful. The creation of a menu to suit one's perceived customers is a type of persuasive writing. This form adds to the other vehicles requested by guidelines in England and Scotland - reports, narratives, letters and so on.

The teacher may feel that additional information needs to be available to assist the pupils.

❖ A discussion on favourite foods and dishes could be used as a possible lead-in.

❖ A selection of recipe books would be helpful.

❖ The children could do some research before the writing itself, visiting food establishments in the area and taking note of the descriptions used and the various devices employed to attract customers. (The descriptions on packaged foods can also be used, and are especially helpful where young children are concerned.)

The tasks

Able pupils are likely to spot key words and phrases that are appropriate for the purpose of appealing to a specific clientele, in the first task. For example, the four different groups of customers are likely to be attracted by phrases such as:

1   'traditional', 'home-made', avoiding exotic terms and foreign phrases
2   'giant', 'jumbo', 'feast', 'double', 'eat as much as you like'
3   'organic', 'fresh', 'low fat', 'low sugar', 'locally-produced'
4   'value', 'no-nonsense', 'home-made', 'inclusive price', 'eat as much as you can for (£5)', 'grub'

All children can attempt the second task, but able pupils should get a great deal out of it as they are given the chance to be creative and imaginative with their use of words. In this way, the exercise promotes individual response or differentiation by outcome through the open-endedness of the work. Alternatively, for able pupils, this activity could be used to achieve differentiation by task, by setting it as a differentiated homework or as a piece of enrichment when the standard tasks have been completed.

The main ingredients for the dishes to be described are given, but others can be added within reason. Clearly this is difficult to prescribe. For example, the starter that is 'a slice of ham with some salad', with the addition of cottage cheese could be described as 'a cornet of ham enveloping cottage cheese, all laid on a bed of salad'.

OPENING UP A NEW CHAPTER

They say that 'writing by committee' produces poor results, but just how well can writers co-operate on a joint venture? Writing on your own allows a number of opportunities and challenges but writing with other people takes particular skill and care. Occasionally in the past, professional writers have written a successful book together. Famous detective writers each contributed a chapter to *'The Floating Admiral'* in 1931. Much more recently, seven famous Irish writers worked together to produce *'Finbar's Hotel'*.

Your task

Below is a short chapter to start off a story. In your group, draw lots or decide between you the order in which you will each write a chapter, with the last person completing the story.

Remember:

- to take clues from the short first chapter
- to continue or end the story appropriately
- to bear in mind your own place in the order and write accordingly

OPENING UP A NEW CHAPTER

Chapter One

The four children, Luke, Margaret, Jenny and Martin, arrived at the home of their aunt and uncle in the late afternoon. They were in poor spirits, as they were not looking forward to their enforced stay with relatives whom they did not know well. Their parents were away on an important business trip, which, if it were successful, would benefit the whole family. As a result the children were determined to make the best of it even though the prospects were not particularly exciting.

Aunt Joan and Uncle Peter were nice enough people and kindly too. However they were quite elderly and they had not had many dealings with children.

Tea was a muted affair with the children rather apprehensive and their aunt and uncle uncertain of what to say. The meal itself was excellent and the youngsters gorged themselves, hungry after their long journey. It was with some relief, when the tea was over, that the children accepted Uncle Peter's suggestion that they should take the dog, Jack, for a walk.

The children put on their coats. Jack bounded about between them, excited about the forthcoming walk. Once outside the dog became very different. He became much more serious. His eyes were set and there was real purpose in his movement. The children felt that they had no choice but to follow him.

Jack led them across open fields and into a dark wood. The air was still and little moved about them, except a rook that seemed to be watching the group intently. The dog kept turning and barking quietly but authoritatively. He approached a dense thicket and his manner became even more excited. This was no ordinary walk. Jack seemed to disappear from view and the children had difficulty finding him. When they did he was at the entrance of what appeared to be a cave leading into a small hill. Jenny led the way, following Jack into the dark, dank cave. The dog had a very clear purpose.

OPENING UP A NEW CHAPTER

Teaching notes

Writing for an audience and writing for a purpose are both involved in this piece of work but for rather unusual reasons. The audience is formed of other members of the writing team as well as the reader. The purpose is to construct a story in chapters, each contributed by a different person, to make a logical and flowing entity.

Writing collaboratively poses great challenges and is therefore suitable for able pupils. The first member of the group has to take clues from the given chapter and develop them, but must leave plenty of space for those who follow. The next writers have more to follow and to take into account but gradually they are looking to move the story on. The last writer in the group brings the story to a conclusion and needs to be left enough space to do so, but not too much.

Practical considerations

1   The group size - it is suggested that each writing team has five members, but this could vary a little.

2   The place of each child in the group - numbers could be drawn from a hat, or the order might be decided within the group.

3   The timing of the work - as only one child in each group is writing at any one time, *Opening Up a New Chapter* has to take place against other pieces of work.

4   The overall plan - either the general principles could be explained and then each child plays his or her own part independently, or a group discussion at the start could be used to decide an outline of the plot and roughly where each child is to reach.

5   An extension activity could involve all but the 'finisher' in the group writing notes on how he or she personally would have completed the story.

Criteria

The quality of the work is likely to involve consideration of:

❖   the analysis of what has gone before

❖   the appropriateness of the chapter

❖   the judgement used in how much space has been left for those to follow

❖   the quality of the writing

If a previous member of the team does not make an appropriate contribution it will make things difficult for the next writer.

   Effective Resources for Able and Talented Children © Barry Teare (Network Educational Press, 1999)

Theme Five: *Numeracy, Mathematics*

Numeracy projects are based upon 45-60 minute lessons. Such lessons normally consist of an introduction, oral work and mental calculation with the whole class (10-15 minutes), work with groups, pairs or targeted individuals (20-30 minutes) and a plenary session with the whole class (about 10 minutes). Concern about the positions of England and Scotland in international league tables has led to demands for more direct teaching and interactive oral work with the whole class and groups, an emphasis on mental calculation and greater stress on mathematical vocabulary.

The term 'limited differentiation' in the 1998 DfEE document *'Numeracy Matters'* caused some unease where provision for able pupils is concerned. However, after the consultation process, the framework does now contain some advice on catering for able pupils. The Scottish paper *'Improving Mathematics Education 5-14'* (Scottish Office, 1997) has retained the phrase:

> *...group teaching arrangements should be used to provide more able pupils with additional challenging problems*

The challenge here, as with the Literacy Framework and indeed with any teaching situation, is to ensure that in raising standards for the majority the needs of more able pupils are not ignored. Given that able children do not need as much practice on some items as the majority of the class do, the time thus saved can be used for interesting examples of enrichment and extension. Indeed not to take this approach would risk causing frustration and boredom.

Working at speed is one of the strategies that can be employed successfully with able pupils. Materials such as the 24 Game (Summus) and 'Countdown' (the maths part of the television game), involve speedy mental calculation, and have been used by the author on the Saturday evening of weekend enrichment courses to good effect. Mental arithmetic is, however, only one aspect of suitable work for the able and it would not figure particularly strongly on a subject checklist of characteristics of able mathematicians. Indeed Ian Stewart, Professor of Mathematics at Warwick University, has made the following comment about Poincaré:

> *The fact that he could not do simple mathematics is not uncommon. Most mathematicians are pretty awful at arithmetic, their minds are on higher things and they are so convinced that arithmetic is straightforward and easy that they are sloppy and they actually get it wrong.*
>
> quoted in *'On Giants' Shoulders'* by Melvyn Bragg
> (reproduced by permission of Hodder and Stoughton Ltd)

Encouraging more frequent use of mathematical terms and vocabulary is extremely worthwhile. *Acute* (page 105) is an enjoyable mathematical game, which involves certain terminology as played in the original version described, and which also stimulates mental agility. If participants develop their own games on similar lines, the range of vocabulary used can be extended.

Mathematics is often learned in small units that are then practised extensively, so pupils get to know which area of mathematics they are expected to use in any one lesson. Drawing from a great variety of areas during one piece of work enhances the difficulty of the task considerably. In *A Calculated Risk* (page 108) and *Board with Numbers?* (page 113), the need to use a variety of opportunities and calculations is coupled with a very definite encouragement to work with many examples of mathematical vocabulary. Having mathematical dictionaries in the classroom is useful for all children but especially for able pupils. The item *Four* (page 73) in Theme Two: **Language Across the Curriculum**, also uses some mathematical terms.

Using unusual settings to pose what are basically standard operations is a key technique to ensure interest and challenge for the able child. *In the Balance* (page 118) requires very basic calculations but the context lifts the demands. Very often solving mathematics problems involves a strong literacy component and this is true of *In the Balance*. *The Year of the Dragon* (page 120) puts the subject of factorials into an unusual and amusing context. Word play is involved and there is also a multicultural element.

Lucky Programme (page 122) puts mathematics into a 'real' situation where a practical problem has to be solved. 'Real life and everyday problems' is one of the required contexts in the Scottish 5-14 Guidelines for mathematics. In all Key Stages of mathematics in the National Curriculum, the phrase 'real life problems' occurs.

Theme Eight: **Codes** contains *Lucky the Cat* (page 169) and *Mosaic* (page 172), which are both number-based codes.

Effective Resources for Able and Talented Children © Barry Teare (Network Educational Press, 1999)

ACUTE

You may well be aware of party games in which the players call numbers in order as they take their turn but in which it is forbidden to say numbers containing a particular digit or multiples of that digit. Instead, there are rules requiring certain sounds to be made in their place.

The Pythagoras Club is a social gathering of six people who have a great interest in all things mathematical. They have made up their own version of this game, which they call 'Acute' because you have to be sharp to play it successfully.

The rules of 'Acute'

1   Each player calls a number (or the term that replaces it) in turn, consecutive to the last one, starting with 1 (or its replacement term), then 2 (or its replacement term), and so on.

2   Instead of any prime numbers, players must call 'potato'.

3   Instead of any square numbers, players must call 'sprout'.

4   Instead of any triangular numbers, players must call 'turnip'.

5   For any numbers that fit more than one of the three categories (prime, square, triangular) players must call 'union'.

6   For any numbers that are not prime or square or triangular, players must call the actual number.

7   Play proceeds in a clockwise direction until an error is made. The player calling incorrectly is 'out' and play changes direction, thus moving from clockwise to anti-clockwise to clockwise, and so on, after each error. Play resumes at the next number after the error rather than going back to 1 (or its replacement term).

8   The last player remaining is the winner.

A particular game

One evening the members of the Pythagoras Club were seated round a table in this clockwise order: Helen Point, Robert Line, Jane Circle, Leroy Rectangle, Susan Cube and Mark Ellipse. To decide who should start, they each threw a normal 1 to 6 dice. After they had all had a throw the person to start was to be any one throwing a 'perfect number'.

In clockwise order, starting with Helen Point, the scores on the dice were: 3, 5, 2, 6, 1, 2.

ACUTE

The record of play was as follows:

> UNION, POTATO, POTATO, SPROUT, POTATO, TURNIP, POTATO,
> 8, SPROUT, TURNIP, POTATO, 12, POTATO, 14, TURNIP, SPROUT,
> POTATO, 18, POTATO, 20, 21, 22, POTATO, 24, SPROUT, 26,
> 27, TURNIP, POTATO, 30, POTATO, 32, 33, 34, 35, UNION,
> POTATO, 38, 39, 40, POTATO, 42, POTATO, TURNIP, TURNIP,
> 46, POTATO, 48, SPROUT, 50, 51, 52, POTATO, 54, TURNIP,
> 56, 57, 58, POTATO, 60, POTATO, 62, 63, SPROUT, TURNIP,
> TURNIP, POTATO, 68, 69, 70, POTATO, 72, POTATO, 74,
> 75, 76, 77, TURNIP, POTATO, SPROUT.

Your task

Work out which member of the Pythagoras Club won this particular game of 'Acute'.

Further suggestions

✍ Try playing 'Acute' in groups of five or six.

✍ Make up similar games of your own, using different rules for numbers that cannot be said.

Effective Resources for Able and Talented Children © Barry Teare (Network Educational Press, 1999)

ACUTE

Teaching notes

The terms

A **perfect number** is an integer that is equal to the sum of its positive divisors (not including itself). 6 is a perfect number (divisors are 1, 2, 3 and 6 and 1 + 2 + 3 = 6) and therefore the first person to play is Leroy Rectangle with Susan Cube next. Play continues up to the equivalent of number 80.

A **prime number** is a positive integer greater than 1 where its only positive divisors are 1 and itself. The prime numbers involved in this game of 'Acute' are 2, 3, 5, 7, 11, 13, 17, 19, 23, 29, 31, 37, 41, 43, 47, 53, 59, 61, 67, 71, 73 and 79.

A **square number** is the product of a number multiplied by itself. The square numbers involved here are 1, 4, 9, 16, 25, 36, 49 and 64.

A **triangular number** is an integer of the form $\frac{n}{2}(n + 1)$, where n is a positive integer. This is best illustrated as shown here.

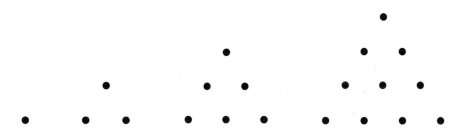

The numbers involved are 1, 3, 6, 10, 15, 21, 28, 36, 45, 55, 66 and 78.

The term 'union' should therefore be used for numbers 1, 3 and 36.

The particular game

If we now look at the record of play we see that Leroy correctly called 'union' for 1 and play proceeded in a clockwise direction, so Susan called next. The first mistake is at number 3 where Mark called 'potato' instead of 'union'. He dropped out of the game. Play then went back to Susan and proceeded in an anti-clockwise direction until the next mistake at number 21 when Jane called the number itself instead of 'turnip'. She dropped out and play returned to Leroy and moved clockwise. The third person to make a mistake was at 44 when Helen called 'turnip' instead of 44 itself. On her departure play was taken up again by Susan correctly calling 'turnip' for 45, and proceeded in an anti-clockwise direction. At number 65, Robert departed as a result of calling 'turnip' instead of 65 itself. 'Turnip' was correctly called at 66 by Leroy, as play was now proceeding clockwise again. The game ended at 80 when Leroy called 'sprout' instead of 80 itself. This left Susan Cube who was declared the winner.

Extension work

Acute uses a limited number of terms. Encouraging pupils to devise other games allows an unlimited range of mathematical language to be involved.

A CALCULATED RISK

Devious Dr Decagon is a brilliant mathematician but she has two major weaknesses - she is very arrogant and she lusts after personal power. The Doctor does, however, have a great respect for other very able mathematicians, including you!

Dr Decagon is being wooed by an organisation called Global Mastery whose only aim is commercial world domination and whose methods are somewhat questionable, to say the least. You represent a group called International Solutions, which is trying to recruit men and women of talent to work on problems worldwide. Dr Decagon would be a great asset to your group in the struggle to save the Earth from inevitable destruction.

True to her character, Dr Decagon has thrown down a challenge to the two rival organisations. She has asked that a representative of each should compete over a series of mathematical problems and calculations. She will join the winning organisation. You have been chosen to take up the challenge for International Solutions but you face serious opposition from Global Mastery: their representative is Professor Prism who has, not surprisingly, two faces - one good, one evil.

THE CHALLENGE

YOU ARE FACED WITH A SERIES OF PROBLEMS AND CALCULATIONS, AND MUST TAKE THE ANSWER FROM EACH PART THROUGH TO THE NEXT. AT THE END YOU ARE ASKED TO CHOOSE FROM SEVERAL ALTERNATIVES AS THE FINAL ANSWER AND TO KEY THAT NUMBER INTO THE COMPUTER. THE FIRST TO DO SO WINS THE CHALLENGE AND RECRUITS THE SERVICES OF DR DECAGON.

DON'T FORGET TO CARRY EACH ANSWER FORWARD TO THE NEXT INSTRUCTION. BE QUICK BUT BE CAREFUL.

ONLY YOU CAN SAVE MANKIND!

A CALCULATED RISK

Taking a calculated risk

1 If the number suggested by the doctor's name is doubled and added to the fourth prime number, and then the cube root is taken, you have the starting number for the challenge.

2
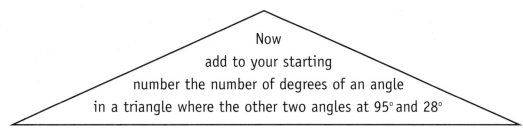

Now
add to your starting
number the number of degrees of an angle
in a triangle where the other two angles at 95° and 28°

3 How many 'score' does that make? (Have you a sense of 'déjà vu'?)

4 Work out n^5 where n is the number you have carried forward from part 3.

5 Subtract from your answer the answer to this problem:

n

> You have a square of sides of n units. If $n = 5$, what total do you get from the product of:
> **a.** the number of sides
> **b.** the perimeter
> **c.** the number of degrees in one of the angles?

6 Don't feel like the number you are working with! Take the 13th letter of the alphabet and use it as a Roman numeral. Multiply that 13th letter by $(n! + 1)$ where $n = 3$.

Add this number to the number carried forward from part 5 and you should be feeling more positive.

D C I V M X L ?

7 Now convert the carried forward number into base six.

8 You are 'probably' ready for this now. Add on the number n, where the probability of throwing a six on *every* one of three consecutive throws of a dice is 1 chance in n.

9 Subtract the two-digit Fibonacci number where the two digits are the same.

A CALCULATED RISK

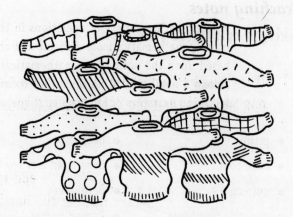

10 Add on the answer to this problem:
The chest sizes for jumpers for 11 friends
are 36, 40, 42, 38, 46, 36, 42, 42, 42, 38
and 38. What is the sum of the mean, the
median and the mode of these
measurements?

11 Now divide the number you carried
forward by the number missing from
this magic square.

4	9	?
3	5	7
8	1	6

12 How do you fancy going round in circles? In a circle where the radius is 14 cm and π is
taken as $^{22}/_{7}$, what answer (numerically) do you get when you work out:

area - (radius + diameter + circumference + number of degrees in a circle)?

Subtract this answer from the number you carried forward from part 11.

ARE YOU READY TO TAKE A CALCULATED RISK?

WHICH OF THESE NUMBERS WILL YOU KEY INTO THE COMPUTER?

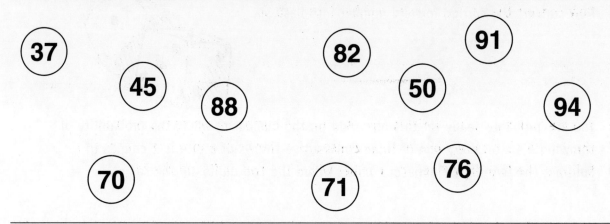

37   45   88   82   50   91   94   70   71   76

A CALCULATED RISK

Teaching notes

Working with a variety of operations in the same piece of work is one way of making mathematics more difficult and challenging. The numeracy projects are based upon the notion that mathematical language needs to be used more, among a number of other important considerations. In *A Calculated Risk* the following examples of language and operations have been included together.

- prism
- cube root
- powers
- negative numbers
- brackets
- digit
- median
- radius
- area of a circle

- decagon
- degrees in a triangle
- perimeter
- Roman numerals
- base six
- Fibonacci numbers
- mode
- diameter

- prime number
- score
- degrees in a square
- factorial
- probability
- mean
- magic square
- circumference

The work also encourages mental agility and alertness. It provides an entertaining way of looking at numeracy. The need to win the challenge encourages speed but necessitates accuracy. Precision of language is another key element as literacy and numeracy so often go together.

Contexts

A Calculated Risk could be used in a number of ways:

❖ as a differentiated homework

❖ as a competition - perhaps two teams in the challenge, or schools in a cluster activity

❖ as a piece of extension work for those well ahead of the majority of the group

❖ as a Mathematics Club activity

❖ as part of an enrichment session

A CALCULATED RISK

Solution

It might be sensible for the teacher to make checks on progress every three or four stages. Otherwise an early error could be compounded and cause frustration and waste of effort. One or two cryptic comments do act as effective checks. Children will also need reminding to carry the number through from stage to stage. The comment about Professor Prism is a reference to the fact that a prism has two 'end' faces with particular qualities.

1	A decagon is ten-sided. 10 doubled is 20. Add the fourth prime number, which is 7, and take the cube root of 27, which is 3, the starting number.	**3**
2	The third angle is 57°. 57 + 3 = 60.	**60**
3	A 'score' is 20 so there are 3 score in 60. ('Déjà vu' refers to the fact that you are back to the starting number.)	**3**
4	$n^5 = 3 \times 3 \times 3 \times 3 \times 3 = 243$	**243**
5	a. = 4, b. = 20, c. = 90. The product is $4 \times 20 \times 90 = 7200$. Subtract this from 243 and you get -6957.	**-6957**
6	The sheet hints that you should now be carrying forward a negative number. The 13th letter of the alphabet is M, which is the Roman numeral for 1000. $n!$ is the notation for a factorial. $(n! + 1) = 7$, when $n = 3$. Add 7000 to -6957 to get 43. A second hint reminds you that you are now back with a positive number.	**43**
7	43 in base 10 becomes 111 in base 6.	**111**
8	The chance of getting a six with the first throw is $\frac{1}{6}$. The chance of getting 3 sixes with 3 throws is $\frac{1}{6} \times \frac{1}{6} \times \frac{1}{6} = \frac{1}{216}$ or 1 in 216, so $n = 216$. Add 216 to 111 to get 327.	**327**
9	The Fibonacci numbers start with 1, 2, 3, 5, 8, 13, 21, 34, 55, 89, 144, 233. (A sequence starting with 0, 1, 1, 2, 3, 5, 8 etc. is produced by adding the terms 0 + 1, 1 + 1, 1 + 2, 2 + 3, 3 + 5, 5 + 8, etc.) The two-digit example where the digits are the same is 55. Subtract 55 from 327 to give 272.	**272**
10	The mean of the measurements (the average) is 40, the median (the middle point of the list in order) is 40, the mode (most frequent) is 42. The sum is 40 + 40 + 42 = 122. Add this to 272 to give 394.	**394**
11	The missing number is 2, so that all rows, columns and diagonals add up to 15. $394 \div 2 = 197$.	**197**
12	In this circle: area = $\pi r^2 = \frac{22}{7} \times \frac{14}{1} \times \frac{14}{1} = 616$ cm² radius = 14 cm, diameter = 28 cm circumference = $2\pi r = 2 \times \frac{22}{7} \times \frac{14}{1} = 88$ cm The number of degrees in any circle = 360. Thus area - (radius + diameter + circumference + number of degrees) = 616 - (14 + 28 + 88 + 360) = 616 - (490) = 126. Subtract 126 from 197 = 71. **Key in number 71.**	**71**

BOARD WITH NUMBERS?

Numbers are certainly not boring - indeed they are incredibly fascinating. Here is a chance to practise and to extend your mathematical vocabulary while, at the same time, using a great variety of mathematical operations. Add to that a link with chess and darts and an opportunity for you to make choices on what you decide to include, and we have an exciting mathematical mixture.

The chess version

First we are going to label the chess board in two different ways.

> ALWAYS REMEMBER THAT THE BOARD IS SET UP WITH A WHITE SQUARE ON THE RIGHT-HAND CORNER OF THE FIRST ROW AS WHITE LOOKS AT THE BOARD.

We can now identify any of the 64 squares in two ways:

1 using a number from 1 to 64

2 using a letter and a number, for example, h6 is also 41.

By following actual chess moves, using instructions involving letters and numbers, we will land on a square with a number between 1 and 64.

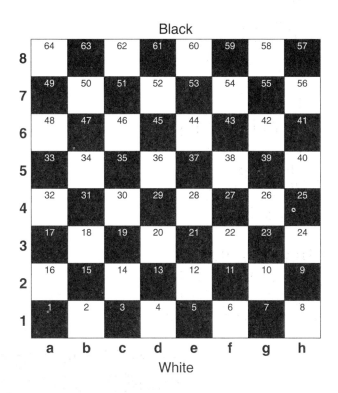

BOARD WITH NUMBERS?

Your instructions

1   Follow the chess moves described below. Note the square from which the piece moved and the square to which it went.

2   For moves by White, find the difference between those numbers (always work afterwards with a positive number). Then construct a mathematical operation that gives this number as the answer, or write a mathematical definition to fit that number. For example, White moves a pawn from a2 to a4 i.e. from square 16 to square 32. The difference is 16. You have to reach the number 16 by means of a calculation or a definition, such as 4^2, for example.

3   For moves by Black, find the sum of the two numbers and then, again, use a definition or a calculation that gives this number as the answer. For example, Black moves a knight from b8 to a6 i.e. square 63 to square 48. The sum is 111. You have to reach 111 by means of a calculation or a definition, such as 43 in base 6, for example.

4   Try to use a different definition or type of operation for each of the numbers resulting from the chess moves. If the same number occurs use a different calculation or definition to the previous example.

The chess moves to interpret

White:
Pawn e2 to e4
Pawn d2 to d4
Knight b1 to c3
Pawn takes Pawn
Knight g1 to f3
Knight takes Knight
Bishop c1 to e3
Knight takes Pawn
Bishop f1 to e2
Bishop e2 to f3

Black:
Pawn e7 to e6
Pawn d7 to d5
Knight g8 to f6
Knight takes Pawn
Pawn c7 to c5
Queen takes Knight
Pawn takes Pawn
Pawn a7 to a5
Queen takes King's Knight Pawn
Queen g2 to g6

Alternative methods

Make your own individual moves or construct your own game of chess and then follow the instructions above. There are many possible variations: you could renumber the squares, or create new rules for deriving numbers or new rules to apply once a number is arrived at.

36 ? 2 ? 56 ? 49 ? 17 ? 8 ?

BOARD WITH NUMBERS?

The darts version

This follows the same ideas as the chess version, in terms of using definitions and operations, but this time you will use the numbers on a dart board.

There are twenty numbers on the board, each having three possible values - a single score, a double score (the outer ring) or a treble score (the small inner ring). For example, in the '19' segment, the score could be 19, 38 or 57 depending on where the dart lands.
There are also an outer bull and an inner bull, which score 25 and 50 respectively.

The numbers in clockwise order from the top are 20, 1, 18, 4, 13, 6, 10, 15, 2, 17, 3, 19, 7, 16, 8, 11, 14, 9, 12 and 5. We can view the numbers as five groups of four numbers as we move clockwise around the board from the top.

Your instructions

1 Throw a dice. Numbers 1 to 5 tell you which group of four numbers you are to use. For example, if you throw a 3, use the third group: 2, 17, 3 and 19. If a 6 is thrown, use the inner bull (50), the outer bull (25) and any two numbers next to each other on the board.

2 For the four numbers generated:
   a. look for a sequence to explain them
   b. give a definition or calculation that gives each number as the answer
   c. work out the sum of the four numbers and construct an operation or give a definition for that total number
   d. carry out a series of mathematical operations to get to each of the four numbers in turn

   Try to use imaginative routes, not just the simple methods of addition, subtraction etc. For example, to get from 20 to 1 you might say 'subtract (2^4 + the second prime number)'.

3 To extend the work further, once you have identified the four numbers you are working with, throw the dice again. For each of the four numbers, a 1 or 5 leaves the number single, a 2 or 4 doubles the number, a 3 or 6 trebles the number (thus replicating the idea of throwing darts into the board). For example, the first use of the dice produces a 5. The fifth group of four numbers is 14, 9, 12 and 5. The dice is then used to decide singles, doubles and trebles. You throw a 2 first (2 x 14 = 28), then a 5 (single 9), then a 6 (3 x 12 = 36) and finally a 4 (2 x 5 = 10). The numbers to use for your definitions and operations are now 28, 9, 36 and 10.

Alternative methods

As with the chess version, there are many possible variations: you could alter the number groupings, the operations to derive numbers, or the operations to undertake with those numbers.

BOARD WITH NUMBERS?

Teaching notes

Many mathematically able children delight in numbers and the manipulation of them. The title is used as a pun but also indicates that the work employs a chess board or a dart board. Indeed, it is important to have a physical example of the board available. This is particularly true where the chess version is concerned, so that children may follow the moves physically.

The instructions are tight and detailed. This is one aspect of the work. Contrasting with that is the opportunity for children to use a wide range of mathematical definitions and operations of their own choice. Mathematics dictionaries are very useful. The requirement to use a variety of definitions and operations takes children right across the mathematics curriculum in this single piece of work, thus making the work more difficult and challenging and therefore meeting the needs of able pupils.

Key elements

Board with Numbers? has a number of features:
- ❖ mathematical language
- ❖ following instructions
- ❖ creative interpretation
- ❖ use of a wide range of mathematical topics at the same time
- ❖ links with games
- ❖ use of a mathematical dictionary

Contexts

There are various possible uses for this activity:
- ❖ in a competition
- ❖ as a Mathematics Club activity
- ❖ as a piece of extension work
- ❖ as part of an enrichment activity
- ❖ as a differentiated homework
- ❖ as a team response during a cluster activity

Extension

As indicated on the pupil sheets there are numerous variations for both chess and darts versions which allow children to take the work on further.

BOARD WITH NUMBERS?

The chess moves

White	Number to use	Black	Number to use
12 to 28	16	53 to 44	97
13 to 29	16	52 to 36	88
2 to 19	17	58 to 43	101
28 to 36	8	43 to 36	79
7 to 22	15	51 to 35	86
19 to 36	17	61 to 36	97
3 to 21	18	35 to 29	64
22 to 29	7	49 to 33	82
6 to 12	6	36 to 10	46
12 to 22	10	10 to 42	52

IN THE BALANCE

Mr Parrot, the pet shop owner, was preparing to employ a young assistant. Susan went for an interview for the job. Mr Parrot wanted to see how well she could cope with problems, so he set her a puzzle. Susan came through with flying colours. Would you have done as well?

Here is the problem

You are selling heavy items like cat litter, which are sold by the kilogram.
The shop has an old-fashioned set of scales, which uses weights placed onto one pan to balance the goods on the pan on the other side.
You need to be able to weigh quantities in full kilograms from 1 to 10 kilograms inclusive.
The weights are in full units of kilograms, no fractions.
You are only allowed *three* such weights and they can only be single figure weights.
Any quantity must be weighed in one operation - you cannot for instance get 4 kilograms by weighing out two lots of 2 kilograms.

WHICH THREE WEIGHTS WOULD YOU CHOOSE TO BE ABLE TO WEIGH QUANTITIES FROM 1 TO 10 KG INCLUSIVE?

IN THE BALANCE

Solution

The key point in the solution is that weights can not only be added together but can also be subtracted from each other by placing one or more weights on the side of the scales where the goods are positioned. For example, 4 kg could be weights of 3 kg and 1 kg added together, or a 5 kg weight on one side with a 1 kg weight added to the goods being weighed.

Various combinations of three weights will solve the problem. Two combinations are given below but there are others.

1   Using 1 kg, 2 kg and 7 kg weights:

Weight of goods	Combination of weights to use
1	1
2	2
3	(2 + 1)
4	(7 - 1 - 2)
5	(7 - 2)
6	(7 - 1)
7	7
8	(7 + 1)
9	(7 + 2)
10	(7 + 2 + 1)

2   Using 1 kg, 3 kg and 8 kg weights:

Weight of goods	Combination of weights to use
1	1
2	(3 - 1)
3	3
4	(3 + 1)
5	(8 - 3)
6	(8 + 1 - 3)
7	(8 - 1)
8	8
9	(8 + 1)
10	(8 + 3 - 1)

THE YEAR OF THE DRAGON

Mrs Radius is the sort of teacher who is always organising interesting and exciting activities in her junior school classroom. She likes her children to be aware of the many festivals and celebrations that take place during the year. Today the class was preparing for 'Yuan Tan' - the Chinese New Year. The children were thoroughly enjoying designing and producing flags, banners and lanterns.

Mrs Radius has a particular interest in mathematics. She decided to couple this interest with the work in preparation for the Chinese New Year. She gave each child two sheets, each containing 12 identical dragons (i.e. 24 in all) spaced out evenly on the paper. Each dragon was divided into four parts - the head, the first half of the body, the second half of the body and the tail. Mrs Radius told the children to choose four colours and to use them to colour the drawings so that they ended up with 24 dragons, each with a different colour scheme.

For example:

1 **Red** head, **blue** first half of body, **yellow** second half of body, **green** tail

2 **Green** head, **yellow** first half of body, **red** second half of body, **blue** tail and so on.

(ONLY ONE COLOUR CAN BE USED FOR EACH SECTION.)

Mr Metaphor, who had many talents but whose mathematical ability was not one of his strengths, saw this work going on. He thought that this was a good idea but he preferred to go for something 'on the grand scale'. He told Mrs Radius that he was going to get his class to do the same exercise but using eight-sectioned dragons and eight colours. Mrs Radius asked him if there was sufficient duplicating paper to run off the necessary sheets of dragons. She had an amused look on her face. Mr Metaphor did not know what the joke was. He said that he had three packets of paper available!

Now, can you answer the following?

- ✍ How could the children in Mrs Radius' class organise their 24 dragons so that no colour scheme would be repeated?

- ✍ Why are there 24 possible different-coloured dragons when four colours are used for four sections of the dragon?

- ✍ Would the three packets of paper be sufficient for Mr Metaphor's purpose? Explain your answer. (A PACKET OF PAPER CONTAINS 500 SHEETS).

Effective Resources for Able and Talented Children © Barry Teare (Network Educational Press, 1999)

THE YEAR OF THE DRAGON

Solutions

1   There are various possible ways of organising the colours so that 24 different schemes are achieved with no repetition. One method is to take one of the four colours and use that as the head for the six possible combinations. For example:

❖ blue, red, green, yellow

❖ blue, red, yellow, green

❖ blue, yellow, red, green

❖ blue, yellow, green, red

❖ blue, green, red, yellow

❖ blue, green, yellow, red

Then use another colour for the head and do the six combinations. If the remaining two colours are then used in the same way, all 24 variations are achieved.

The key point is that the child should show a system, rather than working haphazardly.

2   The first colour can be chosen in 4 ways, the second in 3 ways (since one colour has already been used), the third colour in 2 ways and the fourth in 1 way only. The number of possibilities is therefore 4!, or factorial 4. Worked out, this is $4 \times 3 \times 2 \times 1$, which equals 24.

3   8 colours and 8 dragon sections means that the number of variations is 8! or factorial 8, i.e. $8 \times 7 \times 6 \times 5 \times 4 \times 3 \times 2 \times 1$, which equals 40,320 possibilities. Each child would therefore need to have enough sheets to be able to colour in 40,320 dragons! It is no wonder that Mrs Radius was amused. Three packets of paper contain 1500 sheets and with 12 dragons per sheet this would provide a total of 18,000 dragons - in other words not even half the requirements of one child. Taking a full class into account, the paper demands would be incredible, not to mention the time involved.

LUCKY PROGRAMME

Radley High School was holding an Easter Fair to raise extra funds. Admission was by programme - 20p for adults, 10p for children. On each programme was a number: at the Fair, there would be a draw for the winning number. The person who had bought the programme bearing that number would win a bottle of sherry.

Mr Brown was in charge of programme sales. Some programmes were sold before the day of the Fair. Mr Brown looked after the 'door' on the day, selling programmes to those who had not bought them in advance. The Fair started at 2.00 pm and by 3.00 pm there were no new arrivals. Mr Brown went to the school office to count the money, assisted by the school secretary, Mrs French.

They had just finished counting the money at 3.20 pm when the organiser, Miss Scott, came into the office. She told Mr Brown that the draw for the lucky programme number was to take place at 3.30 pm. Mr Brown realised that he had not made any arrangements for the draw! 'We haven't got enough time to write out a duplicate set of numbers,' he said.

Mrs French asked how many programmes had been sold. Mr Brown explained that a thousand had been printed and that numbers 800 to 1000 were left. 'Don't forget that some advance programmes were returned,' said Mrs French. 'Here they are - numbers 300 to 399.'

Your task

Can you devise a method to allow the draw to take place in ten minutes time? All the numbers sold must go into the draw and the people at the Easter Fair need to feel that the winning programme is selected fairly.

LUCKY PROGRAMME

Teaching notes

Lucky Programme is an example of mathematics being used in a real life situation. It is the problem-solving component that is important rather than the mathematics itself.

With only ten minutes available the method has to be quick to produce and easy to operate. Children may suggest a number of ways of doing this. Often these are rather far-fetched and involve immediate access to computers, software etc. Pupil answers are often unrealistic in terms of time. A useful class discussion can follow.

Contexts

The work can be used:

❖ for individuals as a piece of extension or enrichment work when they have finished ahead of the class
❖ for group discussion and solutions
❖ as a piece of differentiated homework
❖ as a Mathematics Club activity

A possible solution

One simple method involves the use of ten pieces of card or paper of the same size. Each card has a number written on it so that numbers 0-9 inclusive are used. By drawing one card on three separate occasions the winning number can be given.

The original numbers went from 1 to 1000 but numbers 300 to 399 and 800 to 1000 were not sold. The draw must therefore allow any number from 1 to 299 and 400 to 799.

The first card drawn is from the 'hundreds'. Cards 0, 1, 2, 4, 5, 6, and 7 should be used. If 0 is drawn that means the winning number is less than a hundred. The second draw is for the 'tens'. All numbers (0-9) should be included. The third and final draw is for the 'units'. Again, all ten cards should be used. There is one exception. In the rare event of 0 being drawn for both the hundred and the tens, the 0 card should not be included in the draw for the units. Otherwise the number 000 could be produced and there was no such programme.

Theme Six: *Science*

Delivering content in an interesting and challenging manner to benefit able pupils is a key issue in all curriculum areas. In science this is perhaps even more important due to the heavy content requirements. In the National Curriculum, for instance, the subject order for science is almost twice as long as for the next longest subject.

Both the Scottish and English documents have extensive sections on materials and their properties. Key Stage 2 of the National Curriculum states that pupils should:

> *compare everyday materials, e.g. wood, rock, iron, aluminium, paper, polythene, on the basis of their properties, including hardness, strength, flexibility and magnetic behaviour, and to relate those properties to everyday uses of the materials.*

When working on *Property to Let* (page 126) pupils make exactly such comparisons and connections, but in an unusual way. This activity also provides an opportunity for creative scientific writing. Many able children have a strong and quirky sense of humour, which *Property to Let* would fire.

Reports in many curriculum areas, including science, recommend greater use of subject-specific language. This is backed by statements in the relevant curriculum documents in England and in Scotland. The science section of the Scottish 5-14 Guidelines says:

> *At all stages, pupils should be encouraged to learn, understand and use the language, terminology and symbols appropriate to the area of study and their stage of development.*

The presence of subject-specific dictionaries is a boon, especially to able children. *Professor Malaprop* (page 129) explores the correct use of scientific language and promotes the use of such dictionaries.

Ruby Red (page 133) looks at the identification of minerals. It is a lengthy piece. In these days of 'sound-bite' communication and quickfire media presentation it is important that able children work with items that demand a good span of concentration. The data, and especially the tests for identification, involve a number of scientific methods and examples of vocabulary. The higher-order thinking skill of synthesis is also involved, as information from three sources has to be merged. The vehicle is an interesting one.

In the Swim (page 142) again has quite a lot of data. It is based upon a real life situation, although some of the details have been changed. *In the Swim* fits the requirements of the National Curriculum to cover 'science in everyday life' at Key Stage 2 and 'application of science' in the Key Stage 3 programme of study. It is a piece of work that follows the pattern of collecting evidence, interpreting it and acting upon it, described in the Scottish 5-14 Guidelines.

Two other items in Section Three are particularly concerned with science. These are *The Question Is – Science* in Theme Eleven: **Alternative Answers**, **Imagination**, **Creativity** (page 222) and 'Scintillating Science Speak' within *Quintessential Qualities* in Theme Two: **Language Across the Curriculum** (page 71).

PROPERTY TO LET

You have a set of 48 cards. 24 of these are articles that can be found in or around the home. The other 24 represent a variety of materials, both metal and non-metal.

✍ Divide the 48 cards into the two groups described above.

✍ Now match each article with a material so that you finish up with 24 pairs of cards. The material should be suitable for the purpose of the article.

THE PROPERTIES OF THE MATERIALS ARE VERY IMPORTANT. FOR EXAMPLE, PLASTIC IS A GOOD INSULATOR AND CAN, THEREFORE, BE USED ON THE HANDLE OF A PAN.

✍ Write out the complete list of pairs.

✍ Now shuffle each set of cards separately, and deal out 24 random pairs.

✍ For each pair, say whether the combination of material and article could be made to work, and whether it is better or worse than the original pairing. Explain your answers in as much detail as possible.

✍ You could write an imaginative and amusing story based around the random pairs.

PROPERTY TO LET

LEATHER	CUP	SAUCEPAN	PYREX
GOLD	IRON	CAN	PACKAGING
TEA TOWEL	GLOVES	PAPER	BELL
MERCURY	BRONZE	GLASS	TEAPOT
GATE	TIN	PIPES	BRACELET
DISH	CARDBOARD	HANDBAG	SPOON
COTTON	STEEL	POLYSTYRENE	KNIFE
WOOD	BOTTLE	BOX	CHINA
PLASTIC	TABLE MATS	LIQUID IN THERMOMETER	CHROMIUM
TEA COSY	TRIMS ON THE COOKER	TUNGSTEN	CORK
TISSUES	FILAMENT IN LIGHT BULB	WOOL	COPPER
WASHING UP BOWL	SILVER	RUBBER	ALUMINIUM

PROPERTY TO LET

Teaching notes

Property to Let applies to work on materials and their properties. It is an example of everyday science, looked for in both English and Scottish guidelines. The teacher will need to decide what other information is to be made available. If used as a revision exercise, nothing but the pupil sheet would be required, but in other situations pupils would need access to information on the materials used. The sheet of 'cards' (page 127) is printed with the items out of order so that pupils could be given the complete sheet without seeing the 'answers'. It would be helpful to copy this sheet on card.

The 24 suggested pairs are:

- leather - handbag
- polystyrene - packaging
- tin - can
- tungsten - filament in light bulb
- iron - gate
- aluminium - saucepan
- mercury - liquid in thermometer
- copper - pipes
- cork - table mats
- wood - spoon
- rubber - gloves
- steel - knife
- china - cup
- gold - bracelet
- Pyrex - dish
- chromium - trims on the cooker
- cardboard - box
- bronze - bell
- wool - tea cosy
- silver - teapot
- cotton - tea towel
- paper - tissues
- plastic - washing up bowl
- glass - bottle.

Some variations will be suggested and will be acceptable in terms of the suitability of materials, e.g. steel - teapot, or silver - knife.

Pupils will work out their own strategies. Some materials have more than one use, others will only fit one article. Pupils will find it helpful to place first the articles that have no alternatives.

The suggestion of writing an account involving the random pairs is included to give a contrast. A child with imagination may produce a 'Roald Dahl-type' story, thus combining creative writing with scientific principles.

Key elements

Property to Let has a number of elements including:

- ❖ information processing
- ❖ creative writing
- ❖ imagination
- ❖ analysis
- ❖ application of the properties of materials
- ❖ hypothesising

Effective Resources for Able and Talented Children © Barry Teare (Network Educational Press, 1999)

PROFESSOR MALAPROP

Some of you will know about Mrs Malaprop, a character in Sheridan's play *'The Rivals'*. She was famous for getting words mixed up, especially long words. Professor Malaprop is a distant descendant who has the same problem with words. Although he is a very good scientist the professor often uses the wrong term in his notes, as you will see below.

Your tasks

✍ Read the following extracts from Professor Malaprop's notebook.

✍ Identify words that have been used incorrectly.

✍ Decide which words should have been used.

Extract one
The science relating to vehicle movement is fascinating. Speed is one particular feature. Manufacturers are interested in improving the aberration as many customers are attracted by how quickly they can reach high speeds. A linked feature is that of the noise produced. The decimal level has to be considered within environmental requirements. We need to look at the question of fraction to make sure that the vehicle is not held back any more than it has to be.

Extract two
A major development in recent years has been the growing interest in diet and food hygiene. Advice abounds on the essential ingredients for a healthy diet. Carbides play a vital role in the metamorphosis of all living organisms. Sugars and starch are very important. Milk is a good source of sodium to help maintain the health of the bones. Those who have decided not to eat meat need to find other sources of protons. The food industry needs scientific knowledge to carry out its processes appropriately and safely e.g. fertilisation in beer and wine production.

PROFESSOR MALAPROP

Extract three

Students are required to familiarise themselves with a large variety of scientific processes, and the pieces of equipment that go with them. The conditions in which the processes are carried out are important and therefore the parasites need to be noted. The first process for this term is photosynthesis or the passing of an elastic current through a substance in solution or molten form. The students will also be looking at changing gases into liquids by the process of conduction. It would be useful then to look at the reverse process, evolution. A sub-section of work will be aimed at the use of cathodes and their role in speeding up and assisting chemical reactions needed in some industrial processes.

Extract four

Some critics of education complain about the lack of rigour in some of the work asked of students. Perhaps one solution would be to deal with a number of areas in the same pieces of work. That would certainly increase the difficulty and therefore the challenge to students. Could we construct a unit of work linking magnitude forces, and their influences on some metals (and, indeed, on compass points), with divergent sections involving the centigrade forces at work on fairground rides, and a calculation of the complete swing of a pentagon (nicely linking with other fairground attractions)? If we follow the fairground theme, we might, at the same time, examine the science behind stalls where trying to drop a coin onto a prize under water is made more difficult by reflux.

Extension

Write your own extracts, which might well have appeared in the notebooks of Professor Malaprop.

- Sort out pairs of words that have similarities.
- Set them into a piece of writing that provides an appropriate context.
- Have, on a separate sheet, the words that should have been used.

PROFESSOR MALAPROP

Teaching notes

Both the National Curriculum and the Scottish 5-14 Guidelines stress the importance of using scientific language appropriately. There has been criticism that subject-specific language is not used enough. *Professor Malaprop* encourages this, among a number of elements.

Key elements

- ❖ use of a scientific dictionary
- ❖ use of scientific language
- ❖ covering a number of topics within one piece of work
- ❖ application to pupils' own examples in the extension task
- ❖ analysis of text

Extract one

1	incorrect:	aberration	When a lens does not produce a true image
	correct:	acceleration	An increase in speed
2	incorrect:	decimal	A system of numbers
	correct:	decibel	Unit for measuring sound volume
3	incorrect:	fraction	Part of a unit
	correct:	friction	The force opposing motion

Extract two

4	incorrect:	carbides	Chemical compounds of metals with carbon
	correct:	carbohydrates	Chemical compounds including sugars and starches
5	incorrect:	metamorphosis	Change in form e.g. tadpole into a frog
	correct:	metabolism	Chemical and physical processes in living organisms
6	incorrect:	sodium	An alkali metal
	correct:	calcium	Essential mineral in animals: found in bones, teeth, blood and nerves
7	incorrect:	protons	Particles that carry a positive charge
	correct:	proteins	Essential organic compounds for building and repairing body cells
8	incorrect:	fertilisation	Fusion of male and female sex cells
	correct:	fermentation	Conversion of sugars to alcohol

Extract three

9	incorrect:	parasites	Organisms living in or on the body of another organism
	correct:	parameters	Constants or variables that affect outcomes
10	incorrect:	photosynthesis	A process by which plants make food
	correct:	electrolysis	Chemical decomposition by passing an electric current
11	incorrect:	elastic	A material that regains its former shape after deformation
	correct:	electric	The current used in electrolysis
12	incorrect:	conduction	Heat passing through a solid, or flow of electrical charge
	correct:	condensation	Process by which a substance changes state from gas to liquid
13	incorrect:	evolution	Process whereby species change over enormous time periods
	correct:	evaporation	Process by which a substance changes state from a liquid to a gas
14	incorrect:	cathodes	Parts of an electrochemical cell
	correct:	catalysts	Substances that increase the rate of a chemical reaction without changing themselves

Extract four

15	incorrect:	magnitude	The absolute value of a quantity
	correct:	magnetic	Forces originating within the Earth
16	incorrect:	centigrade	A temperature scale on which water boils at 100 degrees and freezes at 0 degrees
	correct:	centrifugal	An apparent force that acts outwards on a body moving about a centre
17	incorrect:	pentagon	A five-sided shape
	correct:	pendulum	A mass suspended so as to swing freely
18	incorrect:	reflux	Liquid boiled so that the vapour liquefies and returns to the boiler
	correct:	refraction	The bending of a light ray travelling from one medium to another

Extension

Pupils are asked to construct their own extracts along the same lines as those from Professor Malaprop's notebook. This allows pupils to apply the principles already learned in an individual way. It encourages further use of a science dictionary. The methods of working adopted by individual pupils are of interest.

RUBY RED

Julie found some work that her brother, Robert, had been doing on the identification of mineral specimens. Robert was a rather muddled worker and his findings were not at all well organised. The specimens were no longer available so that Julie could not inspect them for herself, nor could she carry out any chemical tests. To help her Julie did have some information on identification techniques and a book in which Robert had put crosses against the entries describing the specimens he was using. Julie was able to work out what all 18 mineral specimens were by careful use of the information left by Robert. Can you do the same?

Information available

- Robert's notes - in their muddled order!

- hints on identification

- the information marked by crosses in Robert's book, including a list of birthstones (by the way, Julie's birthday is a week before Christmas)

> **ALL THE INFORMATION YOU NEED IS ON THESE SHEETS.**

RUBY RED

Robert's notes

a Specimens 1, 9 and 11 are yellow (not just yellow among other possible colours)

b I placed specimen 12 on a book and I could not see any of the writing below.

c Specimens 2, 8 and 14 have cube-shaped crystals.

d I scratched specimen 14 with a piece of glass but I could not scratch it with a copper coin.

e My sister should wear specimen 6 to bring her luck.

f Specimens 7 and 10 felt greasy to touch.

g Specimens 2, 13 and 16 were heavy to handle.

h I played at being a magician with specimen 17.

i I crushed specimen 10 into a white powder with my finger nail.

j When I touched specimens 7 and 15 I found that they had the opposite effects upon the apparent temperature of my finger.

k Although specimen 9 was yellow it made a green streak when it was rubbed over a hard steel file.

l I found that a piece of glass scratched specimen 16 but a hard steel file was needed to scratch specimen 13.

m The types of lustre of specimens 1, 5 and 9 could be described as metallic, resinous and silky, although not necessarily in that order.

n When I looked at a book through the glass-like crystals of specimen 18 I thought that I was drunk!

o The remaining specimens are numbers 3 and 4. Neither can be scratched by glass but specimen 4 can be scratched by specimen 3.

RUBY RED

Information about the minerals

BIRTHSTONES

Birthstones are the gems that are associated with the months of the year. It is considered lucky to wear the stone of the month in which your birthday falls.

They are:

January	Garnet	**July**	Ruby
February	Amethyst	**August**	Peridot
March	Aquamarine	**September**	Sapphire
April	Diamond	**October**	Opal
May	Emerald	**November**	Topaz
June	Pearl or Moonstone	**December**	Turquoise or Zircon

MINERALS

Below are the entries marked by Robert. They are the 18 minerals that he examined, described in alphabetical order.

✗ **Barytes** Barytes is a heavy mineral, indeed its name means 'heavy'. It may be colourless or white and there are sometimes tints of other colours. The crystals make an interesting shape known as a cockscomb spur. The hardness rating is 3-$3\frac{1}{2}$.

✗ **Calcite** Calcite is a very common mineral. It is found in all limestone hills. The hardness rating is 3. It is normally colourless but often there are attractive coloured tints. The purest form of the mineral is called Iceland Spar. When you look through it everything appears to be doubled: if you place a specimen onto text, the words are blurred because they appear to be written twice.

✗ **Cassiterite** Cassiterite has a hardness rating of 6-7. It is normally black and it is very heavy. Cassiterite is the ore from which the majority of tin comes.

✗ **Cryolite** Cryolite is a colourless or white mineral with a hardness value of $2\frac{1}{2}$. It is used in the smelting process for aluminium ore. One very strange property is that if it is placed in a glass of water it seems to disappear because it refracts light in the same way as water.

✗ **Feldspar** Feldspar is common in igneous rocks. The crystals may be a number of colours but white and pink are perhaps most plentiful. The hardness rating is 6-$6\frac{1}{2}$.

RUBY RED

✗ **Fluorspar**   Fluorspar has a hardness rating of 4. It is used in purifying steel, silver and gold and in the pottery industry. The crystals are cube-shaped, yellow, brown, green or pink, and more rarely blue, when the name 'Blue John' is used. When it is heated fluorspar gives off a greenish glow.

✗ **Galena**   Galena has a hardness value of $2\frac{1}{2}$ and it is coloured grey. It is very soft and very heavy. The crystals have a cubic shape. Galena is the main source of lead after being smelted in furnaces.

✗ **Gold**   This much sought-after precious metal is coloured golden yellow and has a hardness rating of $2\frac{1}{2}$-3. Its softness allows it to be beaten into thin sheets known as gold leaf. Gold never loses its bright colour or decays. The main uses include coins, cups, jewellery, pen-nibs, and tooth fillings.

✗ **Graphite**   Graphite is a soft black mineral, which has a hardness rating of 1-2. It is used to make pencils and as a lubricant. Graphite is greasy to touch. Because it is a good conductor of heat it makes your fingers feel cold as it draws the warmth quickly away.

✗ **Halite**   Rock salt deposits are made of halite, which is a colourless or white mineral with a hardness value of $2\frac{1}{2}$. The crystals are cube-shaped.

✗ **Mica**   This white mineral is found widely. It has a hardness rating of 2-$2\frac{1}{2}$. It feels warm to the touch because it is a good insulator. The crystals have a flat, flaky structure.

✗ **Opal**   Opal is one of the group of gems or precious stones. It is opaque and the colours are very varied. The hardness rating is $5\frac{1}{2}$.

✗ **Pyrites**   Pyrites has a yellow appearance, which leads to it being mistaken for gold. Its chemical composition is iron sulphide. The hardness value is 6-$6\frac{1}{2}$. Pyrites makes a green or brownish-black streak on an appropriate surface.

✗ **Quartz**   Quartz is one of the commonest minerals. The crystals are six-sided with pointed ends. They are highly valued. The hardness rating is 7. The mineral is tinted in a variety of colours. In crystal form, quartz is very useful in radio and radar equipment.

✗ **Serpentine**   This mineral is part of the asbestos family. Its colour is usually mottled green and it has a hardness rating of $2\frac{1}{2}$-4. Serpentine has the silky lustre associated with minerals made of fibres.

✗ **Sulphur**   Sulphur is one of the few minerals that melt easily and catch fire. This yellow mineral is nicknamed 'brimstone'. It is soft with a rating of only $1\frac{1}{2}$-$2\frac{1}{2}$. Sulphur is used widely in the chemical industry.

✗ **Talc**   Talc has the lowest rated hardness of 1. It feels soapy and greasy to the touch. Its colours are white and green. Talc is used in making baby powder, pottery, paint and paper.

✗ **Turquoise**   Turquoise is an opaque, bluish-green gem valued for jewellery.

Effective Resources for Able and Talented Children © Barry Teare (Network Educational Press, 1999)

RUBY RED

Hints on identification of minerals

Rocks can be made up of both hard and soft materials. They consist of substances called minerals, which have a definite chemical composition. Some minerals consist of only one element e.g. gold, silver, graphite and diamond. The majority of minerals consist of two or more elements. For example, oxides are compounds of metals and oxygen, and sulphides are compounds of metals and sulphur. Each mineral forms a different kind of crystal and the most sought-after are the precious stones or gems. Jewellers make great use of the finest gems - diamond, ruby, emerald and sapphire.

1: TRANSPARENCY

If a mineral specimen is placed over writing on a piece of paper three types can be identified:

Transparent the writing can be seen clearly
Translucent the writing can be seen but not very clearly
Opaque the writing cannot be seen as the light is not let through

2: COLOUR

One of the most obvious features of a mineral is the colour. This can be helpful in some cases but many minerals, e.g. opal, can be found in a number of different colours and therefore the test is not fully reliable.

3: WEIGHT

Minerals vary widely in weight for samples of the same size. This helps to give a rough guide to identification but no more.

RUBY RED

4: HARDNESS

A much more accurate guide when identifying specimens is the hardness of the mineral. Friederich Mohs designed a scale from 1 (the softest) to 10 (the hardest), so that each mineral can only scratch others with a lower hardness rating. For example, flint will scratch apatite but it will not scratch diamond.

1	Talc	crushed by finger nail
2	Gypsum	scratched by finger nail
3	Calcite	scratched by copper coin or iron nail
4	Fluorspar	scratched by glass
5	Apatite	scratched by penknife blade
6	Feldspar	scratched by quartz
7	Quartz, flint	scratched by hard steel file
8	Topaz	scratched by corundum
9	Corundum (emerald, ruby, sapphire)	
10	Diamond	

The scratch tests are carried out with ordinary objects of known hardness - finger nail $2\frac{1}{2}$, copper coin or iron nail $3\frac{1}{2}$, glass 5, penknife blade 6, hard steel file $7\frac{1}{2}$. Thus minerals with a hardness rating less than 6 can be scratched with a penknife and those whose rating is over 5 will scratch glass. Another useful pointer is that minerals with a hardness value of less than $2\frac{1}{2}$ can mark paper.

> HARDNESS VALUES TEND TO VARY SLIGHTLY IN DIFFERENT
> TEXTS. FOR THE PURPOSES OF THIS PIECE OF WORK,
> USE THE INFORMATION GIVEN HERE.

5: LUSTRE

Another useful clue to the identity of a mineral is the lustre i.e. the way in which the mineral reflects light. A *metallic* lustre gives the shine that is typical of a metal e.g. pyrites. Quartz is an example of a mineral with a *vitreous* or glass-like lustre. Those that are made up of small fibres, e.g. gypsum, are said to have a *silky* lustre, whereas a mineral that is made up of thin layers has a *pearly* lustre. Adamantine has a *brilliant* lustre and minerals such as sulphur have a *resinous* lustre named after the resin from pine trees.

The true lustre is only shown up on freshly broken faces of specimens.

RUBY RED

6: CRYSTALS

The shape of the crystals can be helpful in identifying the mineral. Some examples are:

cubes	fluorspar and halite
six-sided, pencil shaped	quartz and strontianite
flat, flaky	mica

Crystals can be colourless, or they may always be the same colour for a particular mineral, or the crystals of a mineral can come in a variety of colours.

7: TOUCH

Depending upon how good an insulator or conductor the mineral is, it will feel warm or cold to the touch. Mica feels warm because it is a good insulator and therefore it does not take heat from the finger. On the other hand, graphite quickly takes heat away as it is a good conductor, and this makes the mineral cold to the touch.

8: CHEMICAL TESTS

A number of tests can be conducted in the laboratory to assist identification. Diluted hydrochloric acid makes limestone 'fizz' because of the calcium carbonate or calcite. The same mineral (calcite) changes the colour of a flame to brick-red. Rock salt gives a yellow flame and copper a blue-green flame.

9: STREAK

Rubbed over a harder surface, some minerals leave a coloured mark or streak. For soft minerals, a porcelain tile or a piece of stout paper can be used but for harder specimens the mineral has to be rubbed on a file. The usefulness of the test varies but there are some very helpful examples. This is particularly true of minerals where the colour of the streak is different to the colour of the specimen itself. For example, hematite gives a red streak although it is black, and pyrites gives a green or brownish-black streak even though the mineral itself is yellow.

There are other cases when the streak is the same colour as the mineral but the shade is different. For example, malachite, a bright green mineral, gives a pale green streak, and the red-brown mineral rutile makes a pale brown streak.

RUBY RED

Teaching notes

Ruby Red is an exercise in logical thinking, information-processing and problem-solving. It uses a content that has an appeal and interest of its own. Using data from different sources involves higher-order thinking skills. The nature of classification is an important element.

Contexts

There are various possible uses for Ruby Red:

❖ as an example of work going beyond the Key Stage (e.g. KS2 → KS3)

❖ as differentiated homework

❖ to achieve differentiation by content by spreading into additional areas

❖ as an item for a Science Club

❖ as a piece of enrichment work

❖ as extension from more normal work on materials and geology

It is important that pupils use the information in the exercise rather than more general knowledge.

Solution

Careful use of all the information provided will produce the following results.

a Specimens 1, 9 and 11 are definitely yellow. Therefore 1, 9 and 11 are sulphur, gold and pyrites but we do not know which is which.

b Specimen 12 is opaque and therefore is opal or turquoise.

c Specimens 2, 8 and 14 are fluorspar, halite and galena but in which order?

d Specimen 14 is softer than glass (5) but harder than copper ($3\frac{1}{2}$). It has a hardness value of 4 or $4\frac{1}{2}$. Specimen 14 is therefore fluorspar.

e Julie's birthday is in December, for which the birthstones are turquoise or zircon (not in the list). Specimen 6 is therefore turquoise and from **b** specimen 12 is opal.

f Specimens 7 and 10 are talc and graphite but we do not know which way round.

g The heavy specimens, 2, 13 and 16, are galena, barytes and cassiterite. Specimen 2 has already been mentioned in c. Galena is the only mineral to be used in both clues and therefore specimen 2 is galena. If 2 is galena and 14 is fluorspar, then specimen 8 must be halite.

h Specimen 17 is cryolite, which 'disappears' in a glass of water!

i Specimen 10 is talc and therefore, from **f**, specimen 7 is graphite.

j Specimen 7 has already been identified as graphite from **i**: it is a good conductor of heat and therefore makes the finger feel cold. Specimen 15 therefore made the finger feel warm. This must be mica, which is a good insulator and does not take heat away from the finger.

Effective Resources for Able and Talented Children © Barry Teare (Network Educational Press, 1999)

k The yellow specimens have been named as sulphur, gold and pyrites in **a**. Specimen 9 is pyrites, which makes a green or brownish-black streak. The use of a file showed that it was a hard mineral. (Pyrites has a hardness of 6-6$\frac{1}{2}$.)

l Specimens 13 and 16 are barytes and cassiterite, as has already been mentioned in **g**. Barytes, with a hardness of 3-3$\frac{1}{2}$, would be scratched by glass, whereas cassiterite, with a hardness of 6-7, would need a hard steel file. Therefore barytes is specimen 16 and cassiterite is specimen 13.

m In **k**, specimen 9 has been identified as pyrites, which has a metallic lustre. From **a**, specimen 1 has been shown to be sulphur or gold. Sulphur has a resinous lustre and therefore specimen 1 is sulphur. This means, from **a**, that specimen 11 is gold. Specimen 5 must have a silky lustre, which identifies serpentine.

n Specimen 18 is calcite, which makes words look doubled and blurred.

o Specimens 3 and 4 are feldspar and quartz. Both are hard but quartz is the harder and therefore specimen 3 is quartz and specimen 4 is feldspar.

To sum up, this gives the following result:

1	sulphur	**7**	graphite	**13**	cassiterite
2	galena	**8**	halite	**14**	fluorspar
3	quartz	**9**	pyrites	**15**	mica
4	feldspar	**10**	talc	**16**	barytes
5	serpentine	**11**	gold	**17**	cryolite
6	turquoise	**12**	opal	**18**	calcite

IN THE SWIM

Mr Grayston and his wife own and manage a very good hotel in Cornwall. One of the many attractive features is the outdoor swimming pool. This is a focal point of interest for swimmers and non-swimmers alike. Mr Grayston is very particular about the care of the pool, which is kept in immaculate condition. This involves carrying out a number of checks and routine duties to ensure that the water is healthy and clean and that the pool and its surrounds remain attractive.

Below there is an explanation of the various checks and jobs carried out by Mr Grayston. Based upon this information, you are then asked to detail the duties that you would undertake on specified days.

> THE INFORMATION IS BASED UPON THE REAL TASKS THAT ARE NORMALLY ASSOCIATED WITH THE UPKEEP OF A SWIMMING POOL. HOWEVER, MANY DETAILS HAVE BEEN CHANGED FOR THE PURPOSE OF THE EXERCISE - COLOURS, TEST VALUES, NUMBER OF TABLETS, METHODS OF TESTING, ETC.

Your task

Mr Grayston is taken ill and you have to look after the pool for five days from Monday to Friday, June 15th to 19th inclusive. Before the 15th, the various jobs were last carried out on the following days:

Vacuuming	Sunday June 14th
Scrubbing the sides	Wednesday June 10th
Algaecide added	Friday June 12th
Topping up	Sunday June 14th
Testing the water	Saturday June 13th

Describe what jobs you would need to carry out on each of the five days. Describe the results and meanings of your tests, and explain the reasons for your actions.

Additional information

- It was very windy on both Thursday and Friday, June 18th and 19th.

- The hotel was full during the week in question.

- It was hot on all days except Wednesday, when there was a heavy thunderstorm.

IN THE SWIM

- On the first occasion you tested the water you obtained the following results:
  a. Five tablets were used in testing calcium hardness.
  b. Four tablets were needed in the alkalinity test.
  c. The sample colour in the pH test was represented by:

  d. The bromine shade was:

- On the second occasion, you obtained the following results:
  a. Five tablets were used in testing calcium hardness.
  b. Six tablets were needed in the alkalinity test.
  c. The sample colour in the pH test was represented by:

  d. The bromine shade was:

The maintenance of Mr Grayston's pool

'VACUUMING'
Every other day the pool is 'vacuumed' to remove rubbish that has fallen into the water. In certain conditions, this job is carried out more frequently - following a strong wind for instance.

FILTER BACK
The filter back is on all the time. 11,500 gallons of water are recycled every four hours.

BACKWASH
Each time the pool is vacuumed, the filter is backwashed. This traps foreign bodies that need removing from the water.

IN THE SWIM

THE WATER LINE

Some unwanted material does not go through the skimmers to the filters but instead clings to the side as 'scum'. Once each week the sides of the pool are scrubbed clean.

ALGAE

Algae make the water go green and murky. This occurs over a period of time but heavy rain or a thunderstorm speeds up the process. Mr Grayston adds a chemical algaecide to the water to keep it clear and clean. This is normally done once a week but after very heavy rain algaecide is used also.

TOPPING UP

Water is lost in a variety of ways - splashing by the swimmers, waste running off, evaporation, etc. In very hot weather, when the pool is used by a great many people, this could mean up to 200 gallons being lost in a day. Rain prevents the need to 'top up' but it does increase the amount of algae in the water.

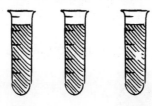

TESTING THE WATER

Three tests are carried out at the same time every fifth day:

1   **Calcium hardness**

   25 ml of pool water are put into a test tube. Tablets are added until the pale yellow colour produced at first turns to a deep orange. The number of tablets needed is multiplied by 5 to give a reading.

2   **Alkalinity**

   50 ml of pool water are placed in a test tube. Tablets are added until the colour changes from light green to brown. A reading is taken from the following table. For example, if 7 tablets are required then the value to be used is 6.5.

Tablets	1	2	3	4	5	6	7	8	9	10
Reading	3.5	4.0	4.5	5.0	5.5	6.0	6.5	7.0	7.5	8.0

IN THE SWIM

3   The pH factor

The pH factor is the correct balance between the alkalinity and acidity in the water so that the purification process can work properly. One pH tablet is added to 20 ml of pool water in a test tube. This produces a colour in the tube, and the colour gives a pH factor reading on a dial. The disc illustrated below uses different types of patterning to represent the shades of colour. The pH factor values associated with each 'colour' are shown.

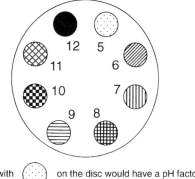

Thus a sample colour which matched with ⬤ on the disc would have a pH factor of 5

4   The calculation

The values given by the three tests are added together. This combined total is then checked against a chart to see whether the condition of the water is acceptable or not.

Combined value	Condition of water
Below 26	Too acidic and corrosive. Sodium bicarbonate should be added to the water.
26 - 30	Acceptable although not perfect. Tests should be carried out on a daily basis.
30 - 35	The ideal balance. No action is needed. Continue routine testing every fifth day.
36 - 41	Acceptable though not perfect. Tests should be carried out on a daily basis.
Above 41	Too alkaline and scale-forming. Add a very weak solution of hydrochloric acid.

5   The bromine test

This is carried out at the same time as the triple test above. One tablet is added to 20 ml of pool water. This produces a shade of blue that is matched with the disc on the right. Any value from 3 to 6 inclusive is acceptable.

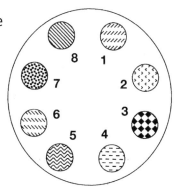

IN THE SWIM

Teaching notes

This piece of work is an example of linking science to everyday life, a requirement of both the National Curriculum and the Scottish 5-14 Guidelines.

In the Swim is based upon actual conditions and reflects the care that is needed to maintain a swimming pool in good order. Some details have been changed for the purpose of the exercise.

Key elements

In the Swim follows a key scientific route of collecting evidence, interpreting it and then taking appropriate action. It also has elements of:

❖ information processing
❖ analysis
❖ evaluation
❖ logical thinking
❖ secondary sources
❖ health and safety

The task

The work needed would be as described below.

Vacuuming	This should be done every other day unless there are special conditions like a high wind. It was last done on Sunday June 14th. It was therefore due on Tuesday June 16th and Thursday June 18th. It would need to be done also on Friday June 19th because of the wind.
Backwash	This would be done at the same times as the vacuuming.
Scrubbing the sides	This was last done on Wednesday June 10th. It is done once per week and would therefore be required on Wednesday June 17th.
Algaecide added	This is normally done once per week. It was therefore due on Friday June 19th. However, there was a thunderstorm on Wednesday June 17th which means that algaecide would be added then. (If the rain came early in the day the work would be done the same day i.e. Wednesday June 17th. If a child says that the work would be needed the next morning, then Thursday June 18th is appropriate.) It would not be done on Friday June 19th as the original schedule suggests.
Topping up	The weather was hot for all the days except Wednesday. The hotel was full and a lot of people would have used the pool. Therefore topping up would be needed for every day except Wednesday June 17th. (Again a child might claim that if the work is done in the morning it would be Thursday June 18th that was the one day when topping up was not done).

Effective Resources for Able and Talented Children © Barry Teare (Network Educational Press, 1999)

Testing

Testing is done every five days. The water was last tested on Saturday June 13th and was therefore due on Thursday June 18th.

The bromine reading on that day was 5, which was within the acceptable range.

The other three scores are added together. The calcium test took 5 tablets and therefore the reading is $5 \times 5 = 25$. 4 tablets in the alkalinity test meant a reading of 5. The pH shade gave a reading of 9. Those 3 values add up to 39. This total meant that the water was in the acceptable range but it was a little more alkaline than would be perfect (36 - 41). This required tests to be done on a daily basis.

The second readings therefore refer to Friday June 19th. Again the bromine reading of 5 was acceptable. The calcium test produced the same result of $5 \times 5 = 25$. 6 tablets in the alkalinity test meant a reading of 6. The pH shade gave a reading of 11. The combined total of those 3 came to 42. From the chart the reading shows that the water is definitely too alkaline (above 41) and therefore a very weak solution of hydrochloric acid would need to be added.

If these answers are put together, they give the daily tasks needed, as summarised below.

Monday June 15th	Topping up.
Tuesday June 16th	Vacuuming + backwash Topping up
Wednesday June 17th	Scrubbing the sides Algaecide added
Thursday June 18th	Vacuuming + backwash Topping up Testing the water
Friday June 19th	Vacuuming + backwash Topping up Testing the water A weak solution of hydrochloric acid needed adding to the water

NOTE: A PUPIL MIGHT CLAIM THAT ALGAECIDE SHOULD BE ADDED ON THURSDAY MORNING, AND THAT THURSDAY IS THE ONLY DAY WHEN NO TOPPING UP IS REQUIRED. THIS IS AN ACCEPTABLE INTERPRETATION OF THE DATA, ASSUMING THAT WORK IS ALWAYS CARRIED OUT IN A MORNING RATHER THAN AT THE END OF THE DAY.

Theme Seven: *Logical Thought*

Logical thinking is of value across the curriculum and in adult life. It is a very powerful tool in making sense of information, deducing from that information and coming to conclusions. It also plays a vital role in many aspects of problem-solving and decision-making.

In some publications, such as Robert Allen's *'MENSA Presents Logic Puzzles'* (Carlton Books, 1996), the contents are designed not to require any special knowledge but rather to achieve satisfaction through tackling knotty problems. There are many children and adults who love to solve such puzzles and problems - others find them infuriating.

Other logical thought exercises can be strongly linked to areas of the curriculum and thus serve the dual purpose of making children think while, at the same time, delivering areas of content in a challenging and interesting way. When well written, such pieces of work make good use of the higher-order thinking skills. Analysis operates through trigger words such as 'investigate' and 'solve'. Where the pieces of information cannot be dealt with individually but rather have to be used in conjunction, sometimes after holding such pieces of data, then the work promotes the key thinking area of synthesis.

'Reason logically' is one of the strategies listed in the problem-solving and enquiry section of the Scottish 5-14 Guidelines for mathematics. Making and testing hypotheses in science involves logical thinking. In the social subjects there are similar processes, which also involve the higher-order thinking skill of evaluation.

Mathematical reasoning in the National Curriculum has strong links with logical thinking. Scientific investigation too is closely associated. Preparing a logical argument and making sense of evidence are integral parts of English, history and geography, among other curriculum areas.

Field and Track (page 150) is a short logical thought exercise. It can be solved by the matrix method but other methods work better for some people. There is some combining of clues to reach the solution.

Food for Thought (page 152) is a little longer and contains more data. Pupils have to hold 'either/or' information until later clues eliminate possibilities. The way that the clues have been set involves literacy/English, and careful attention needs to be given to the precise vocabulary used.

According to the Book (page 155) follows the same principles, but the data is now much more extensive. Synthesis is a key element with the need to combine information from three sources. Again, holding information for later use is a key feature of the work. This particular piece of logical thought has a strong content. Indeed, this technique can be applied to many different areas of content running across the curriculum. It is a vehicle for giving information indirectly, while providing challenge and the use of higher-order thinking skills. An important additional element is the information about some children's books that could be recommended as good reading, especially for able readers.

The final piece, *Radio Six* (page 165), is very different. It is adapted from a real-life example. The amount of information is small and the subject matter is almost an irrelevance. What counts for everything in *Radio Six* is clear, logical thinking and the capacity to make correct deductions.

FIELD AND TRACK

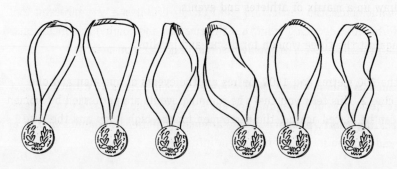

Hartfield is a very successful athletics club, which boasts six members who have competed at international level. They are Tessa, Betty, Jason, Leroy, Susan and Mark. From the clues given below, can you match the athletes with their events?

1 The six events are the 100 metres, the 1500 metres, the high jump, the long jump, the javelin and the discus.

2 The two throwing events were done by men.

3 The two runners are married to each other.

4 Tessa joined Hartfield as a runner but then changed her event to the one in which she gained great success.

5 Betty has known the 100 metres runner for some time - they went to the same girls' school.

6 Tessa's best performance is less than one third the distance that Betty has jumped but they are both great athletes.

7 Jason used to travel to meetings with Leroy until the latter's marriage to the other runner. Now Jason shares transport with the javelin thrower.

FIELD AND TRACK

Solution

Clue **1** allows you to draw up a matrix of athletes and events.

Clue **2** places crosses against the three women for discus and javelin.

Clue **3** tells you that the 100 metres and 1500 metres are the events of one man and one woman. Coupled with clue **2**, this tells you that the jumping events are performed by women and therefore crosses can be placed against the three men for the high jump and the long jump.

Clue **4** places a cross for Tessa against the 100 metres and the 1500 metres.

From clue **5** you know that Betty is not the 100 metres runner but that this event is done by a woman, who must be Susan. This allows one tick and a number of crosses to be entered.

Clue **6** clearly indicates that Tessa does the high jump and Betty the long jump (a little sports knowledge is required here).

The final clue **7** indicates that it is Leroy who is the other runner i.e. competing in the 1500 metres. Mark is therefore the javelin thrower and Jason does the discus.

	Mark	Susan	Leroy	Jason	Betty	Tessa
100 metres	✗	✔	✗	✗	✗	✗
High jump	✗	✗	✗	✗	✗	✔
Long jump	✗	✗	✗	✗	✔	✗
Javelin	✔	✗	✗	✗	✗	✗
Discus	✗	✗	✗	✔	✗	✗
1500 metres	✗	✗	✔	✗	✗	✗

The use of a matrix such as this is one way to solve this puzzle. It is possible to solve the problem, using the same logic, without the use of a matrix.

FOOD FOR THOUGHT

Six married couples had agreed to have a meal together at the local restaurant. They were Tom and Jane, Peter and Christine, Mark and Susan, Andrew and Elizabeth, Fred and Vera and Roger and Kerry. Roger was delayed by a problem at work and he did not arrive until the others had ordered their meals.

That day there were twelve dishes on the menu and, amazingly, each of the eleven people present chose a different meal. They decided to order the odd one out for Roger, believing that he would be happy with the choice.

To tease him for his lateness, the others said that Roger must pass the meals to the correct people without being told directly what they had chosen. To help Roger they gave him clues. Roger himself made it clear that he favoured a meat dish but he did not want anything cooked 'exotically'.

Can you work out which meal each person had and can you say whether Roger was pleased with what had been ordered for him?

The clues given to Roger

1 The two dishes from Italy were chosen by the only two people whose names contain the initial letter of the country.
2 Peter's wife does not like fish.
3 The person whose initial comes first in the alphabet had a dish cooked in red wine.
4 The person with the shortest name said that he came from Burnley and he would support his home county.
5 The person whose name contains a consonant used twice consecutively, chose a dish with the same double consonant.
6 Mark's wife eats vegetarian dishes and fish but not meat and poultry.
7 A person whose name contains one vowel selected a dish that is a 'rival' to Tom's meal.
8 Mark chose a fish dish.
9 Fred's wife wanted a meal involving rice.
10 Jane's religion forbade her to eat any part of a pig.
11 The husband of the lady eating Spaghetti Bolognese chose a meat whose initial was the same as his name.

Food For Thought

The menu of the day

MENU

TROUT VIN ROUGE
Fresh river trout cooked with mushrooms, herbs and red wine

MIXED GRILL
Chop, steak, liver, bacon, sausages, tomato and mushrooms

MADRAS CURRY
A very hot curry with a great deal of exotic seasoning

ROAST BEEF AND YORKSHIRE PUDDING
The traditional English meal

COQ AU VIN
Corn-fed chicken cooked in red wine

SPANISH OMELETTE
A delicious omelette filled with potatoes, peas, tomato and
onion

SALERNO FISH
An Italian dish of cod with a sauce made from white wine, garlic
and chives

LAMB KEBABS
Succulent lamb pieces, tomato, mushrooms, onion and bacon
served on skewers on a bed of rice

ROAST PORK
Served with roast potatoes, fresh green vegetables and apple
sauce

LANCASHIRE HOTPOT
Neck of mutton chops, casseroled with mushrooms and
onions, topped with crisped potatoes

SPAGHETTI BOLOGNESE
Spaghetti with a traditional Italian meat sauce, served with a
sprinkling of grated cheese

PAELLA
A famous Spanish dish of chicken, lobster, shellfish, onions,
peppers and rice

FOOD FOR THOUGHT

Teaching notes

This is a logical thought problem of medium length. The content is based upon both food and literacy, with vowels, consonants, initial letters and vocabulary all involved. One of the important features is that information has to be held and used in conjunction with other clues.

There are a number of ways in which the problem can be tackled. Teachers should be prepared to accept a variety of methods, provided that they are accurate and are not too long-winded. It is interesting to see the working methods adopted by individual children. This means that not too much instruction should be given at the start.

A matrix could be used, although it might not be the most efficient method. Using two lists - one of the people and one of the meals - allows 'possibles' and then 'definites' to be noted. As the problem progresses the number of alternatives is reduced as choices are eliminated.

Solution

Clue 1 Christine and Elizabeth between them ordered Spaghetti Bolognese and Salerno Fish, but we do not know who wanted which.

Clue 2 Christine ordered Spaghetti and therefore Elizabeth chose Salerno Fish.

Clue 3 Andrew ordered either Trout Vin Rouge or Coq Au Vin.

Clue 4 Tom chose Lancashire Hotpot.

Clue 5 Kerry chose Madras Curry.

Clue 6 Susan could have wanted Spanish Omelette or Trout Vin Rouge. Pupils must use the descriptions in the menu given here. As a result, Spanish Omelette is suitable even though in other restaurants it might contain ham or other meat.

Clue 7 Mark or Fred chose Roast Beef and Yorkshire Pudding.

Clue 8 Mark ordered Trout Vin Rouge and therefore Andrew had Coq Au Vin, Susan had Spanish Omelette and Fred chose Roast Beef and Yorkshire Pudding.

Clue 9 Vera wanted either Lamb Kebabs or Paella.

Clue 10 Jane could only have Paella and therefore Vera chose Lamb Kebabs.

Clue 11 Peter chose Roast Pork.

By process of elimination, the others must have chosen Mixed Grill for Roger. He would have been pleased, because it contains a variety of meats and the meal is not exotic.

ACCORDING TO THE BOOK

At Reading Road School there is a small but very successful book club. The twenty members carry out a number of activities - reading favourite passages to each other, writing reviews, doing quizzes and competitions based on books, listening to talks from visiting authors and illustrators and, of course, reading!

From time to time they order new books at a discount price. On one of those occasions the twenty children each ordered one book and their choices were all different. When the books arrived in school one child was absent and could not collect the ordered book.

Your task

By piecing together information from the list of members, the books that were ordered and the clues, you will be able to match up the children to the books that they ordered. The title not collected on the day of the delivery was *'The Tulip Touch'* by Anne Fine.

You are asked to:

- work out which book was ordered by each member
- name the child that was absent on the day that the books arrived

Further points to consider

1 Are you conversant with all the terms that have been used for the children's surnames?

2 Which of these books have you personally read?

3 If you were to buy just one of the twenty books on the list, which would it be and why?

ACCORDING TO THE BOOK

The children in the book club

Peter Page	Peter is an only child whose favourite sport is football. He also enjoys chess.
Lucy Line	Despite her interest in reading, Lucy is an outdoor type enjoying camping, walking and cycling. She has one brother.
Paula Paragraph	One of three girls in the family, Paula has a keen interest in music of all kinds.
Carol Chapter	With three brothers, Carol is the only girl in the family. She likes fishing and gardening.
Vera Verse	Vera has no brothers or sisters. She is an indoor games fanatic and her particular favourites are Mah-Jong and chess.
Ian Index	The youngest of three boys, Ian likes to collect things, especially stamps and coins.
Clyde Cover	Clyde is the elder of two boys and he and his brother are keen footballers and cricketers.
Susan Spine	Susan, an only child, has a number of interests but photography is her real passion.
Terry Title	Terry belongs to the local Archery Club. He has one sister.
Connie Contents	Connie loves going to the cinema where she particularly enjoys watching adventure films. She has one sister.
Simon Script	Simon, the younger of two boys, spends much of his time playing computer games.
Laura Library	Laura, the elder of two sisters, goes to both tap dance lessons and ballet sessions.
Fiona Fact	Fiona lets her only brother ride her horse, Samson, when there is enough time.
Robert Reference	Robert, the only boy in the family but with three sisters, invites his friends round to play computer games.
Felicity Fiction	Felicity, an only child, also enjoys the computer but prefers surfing the net to playing games.
Gerald Genre	Gerald, who has one sister and no brothers, enjoys chess, fishing and swimming as well as reading.
Frank Foreword	Frank has a mountain bike, which is his pride and joy. He has no brothers and sisters.
Pamela Preface	Pamela, the eldest of four sisters, spends much of her time playing tapes and CDs with her friends.
David Dewey	David is a great sports fan, with cricket being his favourite game. He is an only child.
Bob Binding	Bob goes fishing with his friend, Gerald Genre, and sometimes his younger brother goes along as well.

> **PLEASE ASSUME THAT WHERE BROTHERS AND SISTERS ARE MENTIONED, THESE ARE THE ONLY OTHER CHILDREN IN THE FAMILY. FOR EXAMPLE, 'LAURA, THE ELDER OF TWO SISTERS' MEANS THAT SHE HAS NO BROTHERS OR OTHER SISTERS.**

ACCORDING TO THE BOOK

The books that were ordered

📖 J.K. Rowling, *'Harry Potter and the Philosopher's Stone'*
This debut novel has attracted great attention for its action-packed plot and its brilliant invention. Harry Potter leaves his life with miserable relatives to go to wizard school at Hogwarts. The book is full of wonderful creations such as Quidditch, Platform $9\frac{3}{4}$ and The Sorting Hat, and, not surprisingly, was the gold award winner (ages 9-11) of the Smarties Book Prize.

📖 Brian Jacques, *'Redwall'*
A former lorry driver, Brian Jacques had his first book *'Redwall'* published in 1986. It has led to a very successful series. All the characters are animals, but there are very recognisable heroes, such as the mouse Matthias who pits his wits and strength against villains like Cluny, the one-eyed rat warlord. Brian Jacques' fantasy world is the backdrop for incredible battles between Good and Evil.

📖 Theresa Tomlinson, *'Meet Me by the Steelmen'*
Set in Sheffield, particularly the Meadowhall Shopping Centre, *'Meet Me by the Steelmen'* is a supernatural adventure taking Stevie and his sister Jenny back into the past. This magical and mystical story has a haunting quality as it seeks to explain a modern mystery by bringing to a satisfactory conclusion unfinished business from the city's steel-based past.

📖 Kenneth Grahame, *'The Wind in the Willows'*
Published in 1908, this has become a children's classic. Kenneth Grahame originally made up the episodes to tell to his own son. The major characters, all animals, have become friends to successive generations of readers. The adventures of Mole, Rat, Badger and Toad have been favourite stories for so many people, especially with the addition of the wonderful illustrations by Ernest Shepard.

📖 Roald Dahl, *'The BFG'*
This author is incredibly popular with children and his books sell in enormous numbers. 'The BFG' tells the story of Sophie who plans, with the big friendly giant, a way of preventing other giants eating children. One of the many memorable features of the book is the extremely funny individual language used by the BFG.

📖 Philip Pullman, *'Clockwork'*
This is a short but intriguing story surrounding Karl, an apprentice clock-maker who has to make a new figure for the great clock in the town. The sub-title *'All Wound Up'* helps to explain the way in which the larger-than-life characters are wound up into a story that develops in an unstoppable way. This exciting book really is almost impossible to put down!

ACCORDING TO THE BOOK

Jan Needle, *'The Bully'*
Working with a theme close to the heart of many children, Jan Needle develops his plot in a very clever manner to keep the reader guessing. The book is a good read but it is very challenging at the same time.

Terry Pratchett, *'Only You can Save Mankind'*
This is a very entertaining read by master storyteller Terry Pratchett, but it certainly deserves the description 'thought-provoking'. The first of the Johnny Maxwell stories, this is cleverly written and may well have been motivated by the wish to show children that in real life people do get physically hurt and that shooting aliens in games is very false.

Malorie Blackman, *'Lie Detectives'*
Malorie Blackman has written a fast-moving thriller in which her characters are expertly handled. The mystery is well constructed. The dialogue between the children is authentic and convincing.

J.K. Rowling, *'Harry Potter and the Chamber of Secrets'*
The second Harry Potter story carries on from the first, developing some features from the first book but also adding other brilliant creations such as floo powder, spellotape, skele-gro and howlers. Harry's second year at Hogwarts School of Witchcraft and Wizardry is as eventful as the first. The mystery of the fast-moving plot is again constructed beautifully.

Andrew Norriss, *'Aquila'*
A former schoolteacher, Andrew Norriss won the Whitbread Children's Book of the Year, 1997, for this humorous, informative and engaging story. The two main characters, Tom and Geoff, are very much real children. This is a book about hope and determination - the ways in which the two under-achievers cope with all the problems posed by their discovery of an ancient spacecraft, including the need to learn some Latin.

Anne Fine, *'The Tulip Touch'*
This was the 1996 winner of the Whitbread Children's Book of the Year, and you can see why. The numerous, short chapters add to the fantastic pace as the reader is swept to a dramatic climax. Tulip and Natalie play an array of weird games in a doomed friendship. There are disturbing undertones in this powerful story.

Russell Stannard, *'The Time and Space of Uncle Albert'*
This, the first of the Uncle Albert books, marks the start of Russell Stannard's attempt to introduce the elements of physics to children in an exciting and accessible way. The author, a Professor of Physics, uses a fairystory format explaining Einstein's work through the adventures of an imaginary niece, Gedanken. There is a quiz at the end to see if you have understood and then a short section on the 'real science' behind the story.

Philip Pullman, *'Northern Lights'*
'Northern Lights' provides the reader with a treasure chest of delights. This joint winner of the 1996 Guardian Children's Fiction Award and winner of the Carnegie Medal is the first of the trilogy *'His Dark Materials'.* The terrifying plot surrounding fantastic and terrible experiments makes for a compelling read. Philip Pullman has created a brilliantly imaginative story.

ACCORDING TO THE BOOK

📖 E. Nesbit, *'The Railway Children'*
Since its publication in 1906, *'The Railway Children'* has never been out of print - a testimony to the enduring quality of this classic, which was made into a successful film. Roberta, Peter and Phyllis have to solve the mysterious disappearance of their father.

📖 Geraldine McCaughrean, *'Forever X'*
The book is based upon a fascinating idea - the hotel where it is always Christmas. With interesting characters and a strong plot, *'Forever X'* contains thought-provoking ideas on relationships, parenting, the nature of childhood and the view that nothing should last too long.

📖 Melvin Burgess, *'An Angel for May'*
The Carnegie Medal judges described *'An Angel for May'* as 'an atmospheric, eerie book ... it handles a time slip in a completely believable way.' Tam is transported back to the Second World War where he makes friends with May. The characters are very strong in a story that has a powerful emotional appeal.

📖 Gillian Cross, *'Pictures in the Dark'*
Gillian Cross has written an intriguing and powerful book, which has a number of possible meanings and levels of understanding. The link between the photograph of an unknown animal taken by Charlie at night and the strange boy Peter, who causes such upset with so many people, is central to this compelling story.

📖 Terry Pratchett, *'Johnny and the Bomb'*
The third in the series about Johnny Maxwell involves a fascinating succession of timeslips between the 1990s and the Second World War. Terry Pratchett displays his wonderful qualities with brilliant concepts, engaging humour and superb observations of human behaviour.

📖 William Mayne, *'A Swarm in May'*
The hero, John Owen, takes over the ancient position of Beekeeper in a choral school and solves a mystery that has been baffling people for hundreds of years. The boys and their masters are brilliantly portrayed in this magical book, which contains so many layers of interest - the school traditions, the made-up language, the behaviour of the bees and the rich messages of the music.

ACCORDING TO THE BOOK

The clues

1 Two children with the same initials ordered the books by an author who also shares the same initials.

2 The boy whose name means 'the types into which books are divided' chose the book that was published earlier than any of the others.

3 The two books in which all the major characters are animals were selected by children who had no brothers or sisters.

4 The child whose name means not only 'a leaf of a book' but also 'a person who is employed as a personal attendant or who appears at a wedding', chose a book of a single word title indicating 'something running smoothly'.

5 The two children whose initials are the same as that of a group of children (created by Enid Blyton) who 'preferred to be hidden than in the limelight', asked for two books about the same character whose own initials might suggest he is saucy!

6 A girl who would 'appear at the start of a book', and who has three younger sisters, selected one of the titles of longest length, in terms of the number of words.

7 It was one of the children who enjoy playing chess who finished up with a title concerning the fifth month of the year.

8 The boy who has one older brother and no sisters and who enjoys computer games chose a debut novel.

9 Two children whose surnames make a well-known saying (7, 3, 5) meaning 'an exact reference, or authority, giving a detailed explanation', opted for books that involved Sheffield and a timeswitch to the Second World War respectively.

10 One boy used the decimal system of library classification bearing his own name to make his choice, a Whitbread Children's Book of the Year winner, written by a former schoolteacher.

11 The child whose name relates to 'the introductory remarks at the beginning of a book', or can mean 'onward' when it loses a letter but sounds the same, enjoyed his story when he got it, especially the heroics of the mouse Matthias.

12 Books, tapes, reference materials, newspapers etc. make up the _____ (8) of the _____ (7) and the children with those surnames chose books by the same author.

13 A horserider and an angler chose the two books with initials in their titles.

14 This girl's surname would be of interest to the anglers, it would feature in E. Nesbit's 'The Railway Children', and it indicates a boundary as well as being a very small part of a book. She asked for a book in whose title the first word is like her name, once the compass point in the name of the first of Philip Pullman's trilogy is removed.

ACCORDING TO THE BOOK

15 The boy who would 'appear on the outside of the book' and the boy who would be 'consulted for information in a section of the library bearing his name' chose books involving children. One choice is an unpleasant person, albeit a 'challenging' book. The other was selected by this member as a 'river' boy 'warms' (anagram) to his choice.

16 The book in which a photograph is a key item was chosen not by the child whose passion was photography but by the boy whose collections of stamps and coins might be listed by his surname.

17 Many children find Roald Dahl's books enthralling - or another word, made up of 'a magical charm' as might be found at Hogwarts School, and 'the surname of one of the members of the book club' (12 letters). Link this author's book with this child.

18 Connie Contents and Laura Library both chose a title involving the opposite gender, but Connie's book was singular and Laura's plural and not just male.

19 The only child not so far named ordered the remaining title. To help confirm what you have already done you can check that this combination has a link with the author involved in clue **18** and that it is dominated by one particular letter.

Teaching notes

This lengthy logical thought exercise has a number of aims. It involves logic and reasoning and therefore answers educational needs especially at a time when children might be so overwhelmed by accessible data that they forget how to handle it beneficially. Higher-order thinking skills such as synthesis are brought into play as many clues do not stand by themselves and combinations of evidence have to be employed to reach a solution.

Many parts of the clues are expressed in a cryptic form. This involves wordplay and word humour - two characteristic areas of interest for a good percentage of able children.

The piece was written in anticipation of the National Year of Reading. The content is heavily weighted to children's literature and to terms connected with books. As a result there are other outcomes to the work than just a logical thought exercise. The twenty books involved form a rich collection in their own right (write!), and the write-ups also provide interesting bits of information on the authors and on some of the awards for children's literature. Practice in the use of terms such as 'preface' and 'genre' is an added bonus.

The piece is lengthy and complicated. It does therefore require the children to adopt good working methods. Much information has to be held until a later clue clarifies the position. This in itself is a worthwhile skill to practise.

ACCORDING TO THE BOOK

Solution

1   The possibilities are Peter Page, Paula Paragraph, Pamela Preface and Philip Pullman. Two of these children ordered 'Northern Lights' and 'Clockwork' but we don't know which way round.

2   Gerald Genre chose 'The Railway Children'.

3   The two books are 'Redwall' and 'The Wind in the Willows'. Peter Page, Vera Verse, Susan Spine, Felicity Fiction, Frank Foreword and David Dewey are only children.

4   Peter Page chose 'Clockwork' and therefore, from clue **1**, it was Paula Paragraph or Pamela Preface who had 'Northern Lights'. Remove Peter Page's name from the list in clue **3**.

5   Two groups of children spring to mind - The Famous Five and The Secret Seven - but it is the latter who would be hidden (secret) rather than in the limelight (famous). Therefore the children are Susan Spine and Simon Script who chose the two Harry Potter books (HP sauce), but which way round? Susan Spine is eliminated from clue **3**.

6   The girl is Pamela Preface. Two titles with seven words in them are 'The Time and Space of Uncle Albert' and 'Harry Potter and the Chamber of Secrets', but it is the former that Pamela chose, as clue **5** rules out the latter. This also eliminates Pamela from clues **1** and **4**. Therefore, it was Paula Paragraph who chose 'Northern Lights'.

7   The chess-lovers are Peter Page, Vera Verse and Gerald Genre, but of these only Vera Verse has not already been matched with a book. Her choice was therefore 'An Angel for May' or 'A Swarm in May'. This also helps solve clue **3** by removing Vera Verse from the 'possibles'.

8   This is Simon Script, and, from clue **5**, he chose 'Harry Potter and the Philosopher's Stone'; therefore Susan Spine selected 'Harry Potter and the Chamber of Secrets'.

9   The saying is 'chapter and verse', therefore the children are Carol Chapter and Vera Verse. The book on Sheffield is 'Meet Me by the Steelmen' and the timeswitch involving the Second World War could be 'Johnny and the Bomb' or 'An Angel for May'. Clue **7** placed Vera Verse's choice as either 'An Angel for May' or 'A Swarm in May'. Combining the clues means that Vera Verse selected 'An Angel for May' and therefore Carol Chapter chose 'Meet Me by the Steelmen'.

10 David Dewey used the system of his own name to opt for 'Aquila', thus eliminating him from clue **3**.

11 Frank Foreword (forward) selected 'Redwall' and therefore, from clue **3**, there now only remains Felicity Fiction for 'The Wind in the Willows'.

12 The missing words are 'contents' and 'library', and the only author with two books left is Terry Pratchett. Therefore Connie Contents and Laura Library chose 'Only You can Save Mankind' and 'Johnny and the Bomb', but which way round?

13 Fiona Fact is the horserider. Carol Chapter, Gerald Genre and Bob Binding like fishing, but the only angler remaining is Bob Binding. Therefore Fiona Fact and Bob Binding chose 'Forever X' and 'The BFG', but which way round?

14 Lucy Line answers the various meanings and if we remove N for North ('Northern Lights') we get 'Lie Detectives'.

15 Clyde Cover and Robert Reference fit the clues (some may wonder about Terry Title perhaps, but the later information makes it clear). The unpleasant person is 'The Bully'. 'Warms' makes 'Swarm' and a 'river' boy would be Clyde. Therefore Clyde Cover selected 'A Swarm in May' and Robert Reference chose 'The Bully'.

16 The book in question is 'Pictures in the Dark' and it was ordered not by Susan Spine but by Ian Index (this also removes any lingering doubt about Robert Reference in clue **15**).

17 The word is 'spellbinding', so Roald Dahl's book 'The BFG' was selected by Bob Binding, and from clue **13** we know that Fiona Fact chose 'Forever X'.

18 From clue **12** we already know that the two books are 'Only You can Save Mankind' and 'Johnny and The Bomb'. Connie Contents asked for 'Johnny and the Bomb' (singular) and Laura Library 'Only You can Save Mankind' (plural and not just male).

19 The remaining child is Terry Title and the only book left is 'The Tulip Touch'. The author link is Terry (Title and Pratchett) and both child and book use the initial letter T exclusively.

Thus the complete list is:

Peter Page	'Clockwork'
Lucy Line	'Lie Detectives'
Paula Paragraph	'Northern Lights'
Carol Chapter	'Meet Me by the Steelmen'
Vera Verse	'An Angel for May'
Ian Index	'Pictures in the Dark'
Clyde Cover	'A Swarm in May'
Susan Spine	'Harry Potter and the Chamber of Secrets'
Terry Title	'The Tulip Touch'
Connie Contents	'Johnny and the Bomb'
Simon Script	'Harry Potter and the Philosopher's Stone'
Laura Library	'Only You can Save Mankind'
Fiona Fact	'Forever X'
Robert Reference	'The Bully'
Felicity Fiction	'The Wind in the Willows'
Gerald Genre	'The Railway Children'
Frank Foreword	'Redwall'
Pamela Preface	'The Time and Space of Uncle Albert'
David Dewey	'Aquila'
Bob Binding	'The BFG'

The title uncollected on the day of delivery was 'The Tulip Touch' and therefore the absent child was Terry Title.

RADIO SIX

The local radio station runs a phone-in quiz on a Friday afternoon, which takes the form of six questions on matters of general interest. The same questions are put to each of the contestants. The presenter of the programme announces how many correct answers each contestant has given without saying which ones they are. This continues until somebody gets all six right (or if time runs out, the person with most answers correct wins the prize). One particular afternoon the first five contestants' answers (in question order) were as shown below.

	Contestant A	Contestant B	Contestant C	Contestant D	Contestant E
1	gold	silver	gold	gold	silver
2	leopard	tiger	lion	lion	lion
3	metre	metre	yard	metre	metre
4	radius	radius	radius	radius	circumference
5	Adelaide	Adelaide	Melbourne	Melbourne	Adelaide
6	daffodil	tulip	tulip	tulip	tulip

The presenter had, by this stage of the programme, explained that each of the contestants had given four correct answers only, apart from contestant D who had been right with five answers out of six. Given this information (and with a little time to be able to use it) contestant F should have been capable of giving all six correct answers without even hearing the questions! Can you do the same?

Effective Resources for Able and Talented Children © Barry Teare (Network Educational Press, 1999)   165

Solution

A good way in to this problem is to use the answers given by contestant **D**, of which five were correct. Try each of them in turn as the possible wrong answer and see how that would affect the other contestants' responses.

If gold is wrong	**A** would have gold, leopard, Adelaide and daffodil wrong and this cannot be.
If lion is wrong	**A** might have only Adelaide and daffodil wrong, **B** might have only silver and Adelaide wrong, **C** might have only lion and yard wrong, but **E** would have silver, lion, circumference and Adelaide wrong and this cannot be.
If metre is wrong	**A** would have leopard, metre, Adelaide and daffodil wrong and this cannot be.
If radius is wrong	**A** would have leopard, radius, Adelaide and daffodil wrong and this cannot be.
If Melbourne is wrong	**A** could have only leopard and daffodil wrong, **B** could have only silver and tiger wrong, **C** could have only yard and Melbourne wrong, **E** could have only silver and circumference wrong. This answers the conditions.

It is worth checking out the other possible situation:

If tulip is wrong:	**A** could have only leopard and Adelaide wrong, but **B** would have silver, tiger, Adelaide and tulip wrong, and that cannot be.

It is confirmed, therefore, that the wrong answer from contestant **D** was Melbourne, which should have been Adelaide.

The six correct answers were therefore gold, lion, metre, radius, Adelaide and tulip.

Children have found other routes to the solution than the one detailed above.

 Effective Resources for Able and Talented Children © Barry Teare (Network Educational Press, 1999)

Theme Eight: *Codes*

There are many good reasons for using codes with able children. They can be of considerable difficulty. Able children are not always challenged sufficiently. Sometimes they go through their schooling without any real failure. This is not good for the child. Achieving well too easily can lead to not having to develop learning skills. Later, perhaps at university, the child has no strategy to fall back upon when the work becomes considerably more difficult. Most people maintain a reasonable balance of success and failure. Too much failure destroys confidence and the child then needs considerable support. No failure is also bad news. Those who succeed easily until they are young adults can then be badly damaged by a failure, which is outside their experience.

Even if failure does not lead to a traumatic episode, there are other good reasons why constant success is worrying. If a pupil obtains nothing but top marks and complimentary comments, where is the challenge? How does the pupil progress?

Lucky the Cat (page 169), a number code, is not too taxing once the critical route in is found. It is a useful lesson in reading the data carefully.

Mosaic (page 172) is a very difficult code. Indeed, many teachers fail to solve it during INSET sessions. It certainly provides a severe challenge.

Decoding is a trial-and-error process. It is possible to go round in circles. Good working habits are encouraged by having to record carefully the routes taken, and their results. The Scottish 5-14 Guidelines in mathematics want pupils to:

> *work systematically in approaching investigations, problems and routine applications.*

Codes are abstract and, as such, they match one of the key characteristics of many able children. Varying the context and style of a code can increase or decrease the abstract quality of the work.

Some codes, like *Mosaic*, have a strong mathematical element. In any case, codes generally answer certain aspects of the National Curriculum in mathematics, which state that pupils should be given opportunities to:

> *... work on problems that pose a challenge.*
>
> (KS3 and KS4, AT1)

> *... make conjectures and hypotheses, designing methods to test them and analysing results to see whether they are valid.*
>
> (KS3 and KS4, AT1)

> *... appreciate the use of letters to represent unknowns.*
>
> (KS3 and KS4, AT2)

In codes such as *Mosaic* one of the desired contexts of the mathematics section of the Scottish 5-14 Guidelines is met:

> *... problems and investigations where the structure of mathematics itself provides the setting.*

Codes can also support and explore other areas of the curriculum. In *'Effective Provision for Able and Talented Children'* (Network Educational Press, 1997), the author included an activity called *A Capital Idea* in the small number of pieces used as examples. Here the solution of the coded message was achieved by application of the correct and incorrect use of capital letters. This is a vital area of English but not a particularly exciting one to teach. *A Capital Idea* was written to provide challenging enrichment material stemming from a standard topic.

Crossedwords (page 176) is another example of a code that has a word base rather than a number base. It uses a common format, a crossword, but in a rather unusual way.

The final piece in this theme is *The Way the Wind Blows* (page 179). This activity can perhaps be best described as a 'hybrid', in that deduction, observation and word play are all employed.

Effective Resources for Able and Talented Children © Barry Teare (Network Educational Press, 1999)

LUCKY THE CAT

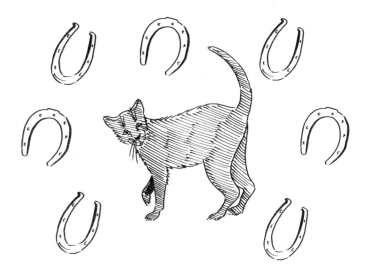

Ron and Beth love to visit their grandmother, partly because they enjoy playing with her cat, Lucky, and partly because she entertains them with games and puzzles.

One day when they arrived she presented them with a coded message. At first the children said that they were unable to solve it but their grandmother helped them by saying that both of their names were in the message, which also contained the cat's name. With this additional information Ron and Beth cracked the code and worked out the message. Can you do the same?

Here is grandmother's coded message:

7-8-2-11-14	26-9-25	2-9-8-13-26-22	9	12-6-8-25-18	24-1
22-26-18	13-9-23-10-18-1	26-18	15-9-1-22-25	14-6-8	
23-6-1 9-1-10	5-18-22-26	22-6	25-18-18	24-22	

LUCKY THE CAT

Teaching notes

Codes come in 'all shapes and sizes'. *Lucky the Cat* is a number code in which the numbers 1 to 26 have been allocated to a letter on a random basis. This would normally make the code difficult to solve and certainly be more complicated than when a pattern is used. However, in this example that is not the case. Even without grandmother's additional information, the children could tease out the solution by using the frequency of letters, common sense and trial-and-error. With the advice that both the children's names and the cat's name are in the message, the solver has a simpler way in.

'Lucky' appears in the message. There are three words with five letters and one of them must stand for 'Lucky':

7-8-2-11-14   or   12-6-8-25-18   or   15-9-1-22-25

'Beth' appears in the message and there is only one four-letter word. Therefore:
5-18-22-26 = Beth

Also, since 'Lucky' has none of the same letters as 'Beth', you now know that:
7-8-2-11-14 = Lucky

If all the letters now known are placed, you will see that 6 must stand for 'O' in 'you', and therefore:

23-6-1 = Ron

When the new letters are placed, a process of common sense and trial-and-error will lead to the complete solution, which is:

7	8	2	11	14		26	9	25		2	9	8	13	26	22
L	U	C	K	Y		H	A	S		C	A	U	G	H	T

9		12	6	8	25	18		24	1		22	26	18
A		M	O	U	S	E		I	N		T	H	E

13	9	23	10	18	1		26	18		15	9	1	22	25
G	A	R	D	E	N		H	E		W	A	N	T	S

14	6	8		23	6	1		9	1	10		5	18	22	26
Y	O	U		R	O	N		A	N	D		B	E	T	H

22	6		25	18	18		24	22
T	O		S	E	E		I	T

Children who race in without taking note of all the data tend to get involved in the more lengthy forms of solution. Some try to apply a code that they already know without acknowledging that it is not making sense. This provides a good lesson in reading the sheet carefully and using all the data. Able children are not always good at doing that.

Extension work

1   Pupils could be asked to write their own messages using the *Lucky the Cat* code. First they will need to allocate numbers to letters not used in the message, while taking care that they do not duplicate numbers already there. It is interesting to see how they set about this task to avoid using the same number twice.

2   Pupils could create their own codes, either number-based, or with a different base. Many able children are very creative and imaginative in this work.

MOSAIC

Agent Smith had been carrying out undercover tasks in a dangerous part of the city. When his contact, Agent Jones, visited his flat one day she found the place deserted and there were obvious signs that Agent Smith had left in a hurry. Agent Jones made a search and found a handwritten sheet resembling a mosaic pattern amongst some papers dealing with floor coverings and furnishings. Back at headquarters Agent Jones showed the sheet to her departmental leader. They were both convinced that a message was hidden in the pattern. The departmental leader showed Agent Jones the most recent coding instructions that Agent Smith had memorised ready for use. Agent Jones was given the task of decoding the message.

Your tasks

✐ By using the latest coding instructions, together with the mosaic sheet, work out what message Agent Smith had left for his contact to find. In other words, carry out the job that the departmental leader had asked Agent Jones to carry out.

✐ Set other messages using the same mosaic code.

✐ Try to design a code of your own in a mosaic format, which could be solved in conjunction with coding instructions.

The latest coding instructions

1   Key word - a rectangle with four equal sides.
2   26 into 25 won't work so two must go together. Common sense will tell you whether it is iob or job.
3   Key number - this is the key word root of the spaces available, indicated in point 2.

EVEN THE CODING INSTRUCTIONS WERE STATED THROUGH CLUES TO AVOID SOMEBODY UNDERSTANDING THEM BY HAVING A QUICK GLIMPSE OF THE SHEET.

Hint

Agent Jones found that her solution of the message was assisted by something she had remembered from a coding lecture during her training. If you get really stuck ask for this hint to help you.

MOSAIC SHEET

MOSAIC

Teaching notes

As with all code work, success in this exercise comes from a combination of interpreting the information well and a trial-and-error process. The teacher has the difficult task of deciding when to help children by supplying extra clues. Obviously, where possible the pupils should work it out for themselves.

The pupil sheet explains that a hint can be given. There are two extra pieces of information:

1   A common form of code is a 5 × 5 square in which each letter is referred to by the co-ordinate for the square in which the letter is located. Since there are 26 letters, but only 25 squares, I and J are placed together. The co-ordinate is formed from the row and column of the letter's position.

2   If that is not enough help, the pupils can be told that the small mosaic grid on the pupil sheet spells out a word strongly connected with the exercise - 'mosaic'.

Solution

Clue 1:   The key word is square.

Clue 2:   Two letters have to go together to fit a 26-letter alphabet into 25 spaces. 'Iob or Job' indicates that I and J go together, and the decoder uses common sense to decide which of the letters best suits a word.

Clue 3:   The key number is 5 because 'the key word root of the spaces available' means 'the square root of 25'.

We are therefore looking for a code involving the number 5 and a square. The Mosaic Sheet shows several rows, each with one block of five squares divided off from a second block of five squares. The letters must therefore be represented by the two blocks of five, giving 25 possible variations if one starts from the viewer's left each time.

The actual code works as follows. A is the first letter in the first group, so one square is shaded in the first block and one square in the second block. B is the second letter in the first group of five letters, and therefore two squares in the first group are shaded and one square in the second group. F is the sixth letter of the alphabet and therefore is the first letter of the second set of five letters: for F, one square is shaded in the first block and two squares in the second block. In this way, using the same shading for both I and J, 26 letters are fitted into 25 variations. The last letter Z is the fifth letter in the fifth group of five letters and therefore five squares are shaded in both blocks.
Thus:

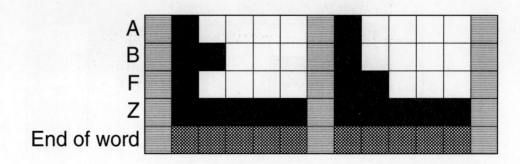

Effective Resources for Able and Talented Children © Barry Teare (Network Educational Press, 1999)

MOSAIC

If this is applied to the Mosaic Sheet, assuming the patterned lines are used as word dividers, then the following message emerges.

2/2	4/3	3/3	5/1		4/4	4/3		3/2	4/3	5/4	3/4	5/1
G	O	N	E		T	O		H	O	U	S	E

4/3	3/3		4/1	4/2	3/3	2/2	1/3	5/1		2/4	4/3	1/1	4/1
O	N		D	I	N	G	L	E		R	O	A	D

CROSSEDWORDS

 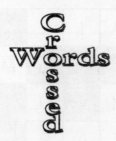 

Even secret agents have hobbies and pastimes - perhaps a necessary release from the tensions of the job. Charlotte spent much of her spare time solving and setting crosswords. Her partner, Richard, preferred outdoor pursuits like golf and fishing.

The two agents are currently on an assignment abroad. They have been posing as sales staff from an electrical company. Charlotte and Richard always agree a particular place within a room where cryptic messages are left for each other i.e. messages that would look innocent to outsiders, but which would convey information to the partner agent.

On one occasion when Richard called at Charlotte's hotel room, she was not present as expected but, instead, there were two items in the drawer that had been agreed as the 'message-holder'.

One was a handwritten sheet of paper entitled 'Thought for the Day'.

Thought for the Day

In life we have to start at the bottom and work our way upwards. It is important that we act from what we believe is right, as we see it. That comes first. Other considerations may have to be left until later.

The second item was the solution to a crossword with the accompanying clues. Richard's suspicions were raised immediately. This puzzle was far smaller than Charlotte normally set and well below her usual standard. When he started to look at the clues and their answers in the crossword, Richard's suspicions were confirmed. He took both items and returned to a safe location. There he worked on both items to decipher Charlotte's message. Immediately afterwards he left the city and hurried to a fallback meeting place some sixty miles away.

Your tasks

✍ Use the 'Thought for the Day' and the crossword solution with its clues to work out Charlotte's coded message.

✍ Explain why Richard did not wait any longer but, instead, hurried to the reserve meeting point.

✍ How did Richard know that the crossword was not set by Charlotte as a normal leisure activity?

CROSSEDWORDS

	¹T	²R	A	I	L			³A	
⁴L		I			⁵M	A	S	⁶T
⁷A	R	C	⁸H		⁹U			E
T		¹⁰H	E	A	P			A
¹¹C	¹²D		N			¹³L	¹⁴E	A	K
¹⁵H	O	U	S	E			G	
	O				¹⁶L	O	G		¹⁷H
¹⁸T	R	¹⁹I	²⁰B	²¹E			²²G	O
U		²³N	U	T		²⁴O		L
²⁵B	E	N	D		²⁶P	R	I	D	E

Clues

Across

1   On the tracks, either as transport or thought (5)
5   Nearly all (4)
7   Chief curved support for a bridge (4)
10   To assist or aid (4)
11   Compact form of compact disc (2)
13   Court slang on the bird's face (4)
15   Information from this animal's mouth is regarded as reliable (5)
16   This limb is one stage of a race (3)
18   United by social, economic, religious or blood ties (5)
22   Monopoly salary for this move (2)
23   A hard one to crack! (3)
25   A uniting force for 007 (4)
26   The cost (5)

Down

2   Poor opposites (4)
3   Green grass needs two of these to make a saying (2)
4   Look at your timepiece (5)
6   As hard as (4)
8   Female birds (4)
9   Not down (2)
12   Leaving this open ensures that an option remains available (4)
14   A product of 8 down (3)
17   A plant-eating rodent (4)
18   A clumsy slow boat provides a bath (3)
19   No room here for Mary and Joseph (3)
20   Later becomes a flower or leaf (3)
21   A visitor from outer space (2)
24   The alternative (2)

CROSSEDWORDS

Teaching notes

Codes can be developed from a number of different bases. *Crossedwords*, as the title implies, is very much a word code but not the normal type. Indeed one of the benefits of this piece of work is that it gives crossword practice and insight while providing an opportunity for logical thinking.

✍ Solving the coded message

The 'Thought for the Day' provides the order for taking particular letters. It indicates that you work from the bottom of the puzzle to the top and also from right to left as you look at the crossword answer.

The letters to use are found by checking the clues against their answers and identifying incorrect entries. Many of the words are appropriate but ten entries are incorrect by one letter. Reading, as indicated by the 'Thought for the Day', from bottom to top and right to left, as the viewer sees it, these ten 'mistakes' are:

1	pride	pri**c**e (26 across)
2	bend	b**o**nd (25 across)
3	hole	**v**ole (17 down)
4	log	le**g** (16 across)
5	house	ho**r**se (15 across)
6	leak	**b**eak (13 across)
7	heap	hel**p** (10 across)
8	mast	m**o**st (5 across)
9	latch	**w**atch (4 down)
10	trail	trai**n** (1 across)

When the correct answers to clues are inserted, the changed letters, in order as indicated above, spell:

'cover blown'

✍
Knowing that their cover was blown, i.e. their identities had been discovered, Richard would not hesitate to leave the city and to travel to meet Charlotte at the new location.

✍
Given that Charlotte was good at crosswords, this would be a very poor effort in the following ways:

❖ It is rather small.

❖ The words are all short.

❖ There are too many spaces blocked out.

❖ The clues are rather too easy to solve.

Effective Resources for Able and Talented Children © Barry Teare (Network Educational Press, 1999)

THE WAY THE WIND BLOWS

The author, Andromeda Andrews, is not only a very successful writer but also a connoisseur of puzzles and codes. When she was invited to address a book club meeting in Stranraer she left the members with the start of a short story that contained a coded message. To help them, she added a page called 'Author's Notes', which contained some clues. This is reproduced below.

Author's notes

1 There is a classical solution but there are other ways of getting to the answer.

2 The title might not fit the story but it does have a part to play.

3 The characters seem out of place but not for my theme.

4 The odd-length lines are not the result of a malfunction on my computer but, rather, a deliberate ploy.

5 Crossword clue: 'The important member of the Roman Catholic Church indicates the way' (3, 8, 6).

6 Cryptic clue: 'If the direction of the instructions make **NEWS**, this would be the same as saying that the main characters initially would describe the type of stalk that Jack climbed!' (where the last letter of the alphabet was replaced by the first).

Your task

With the help of Andromeda's clues, find the coded message hidden within *The Way the Wind Blows*. The first correct solution from the book club members in Stranraer was by Homer Harvey, who told Andromeda that the puzzle had been 'a breeze'. The author appreciated Homer's sense of humour, as you will do when you crack this story code.

THE WAY THE WIND BLOWS

The start of the short story

The Way the Wind Blows

The alarm clock sounded shrilly on the dressing table next to the bed. Eurus wanted to ignore it

but he knew that the others would be waiting for him. He rose slowly and started to get dressed.

There was time for a little breakfast. He remembered to put on his watch. Zephyrus had given

him this as a birthday present. Eurus ignored the wailing of the cat in the back garden. When

was Zephyrus due to arrive? He was not sure. Eurus turned the key in the door and went

to wait on the pavement outside his house.

Meanwhile preparations were going ahead on the other side of town.

Notus was making sandwiches for

later in the day. He, Zephyrus, and others of their assault team enjoyed meat content, but there

were others who

did not, the vegetarians like

Boreas, his brother.

Notus began to think

over the timetable of events. Eurus wanted a good result this time. In the team's plan Zephyrus

was to

take the leading role.

Boreas was to play a flexible part, seeing where the need was greatest. In a rush, Zephyrus

could

make mistakes.

Notus believed that they could do well

even though there had been problems over basic communications before. Eurus watched

carefully for gaps that needed to be filled but

it was not always possible to use

Boreas to best advantage when Zephyrus was 'on a charge'.

Notus sat

down to make the final preparations for the proposed route ...

THE WAY THE WIND BLOWS

Teaching notes

This is not a number code, nor a word code. Some word play is involved. Observation, deduction and interpretation of cryptic information all play a part.

Interpretation of the author's notes

1, 3 Classical knowledge would help in that the characters in the short story are the four winds:

Boreas - North
Notus - South
Eurus - East
Zephyrus - West

Some children might look the names up although there is no obvious reason for doing so.
Their names do seem strange but they do fit the theme of winds and their directions.

2 The title does not seem an obvious one for the content of the story, although this is only the start and later developments might have been linked. The real point is to suggest the theme of winds and their directions.

4 This is an important clue. The passage looks very peculiar but it has been written in this way so that certain words are directly above or below others. Observant children will see that the names of Boreas and Notus only ever occur at the start of a line. This is to make sure that there is a letter directly above or below the first letter of their names. Here is another suggestion of 'direction'.

5 The solution of the crossword clue is 'the cardinal points'. This refers to the main directions on a compass or a weathervane.

6 The cryptic clue tells us which character is linked with which direction and wind. The great majority of children will not know the classical references and will therefore need this clue.

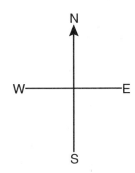

Jack climbed a beanstalk. The 'A' in 'bean' has to be replaced by 'Z' making **BEZN**. We now have:

NEWS = BEZN

Or:

North = **B**oreas
East = **E**urus
West = **Z**ephyrus
South = **N**otus

A combination of clues from the author's notes leads to the solution. Wherever the four characters' names appear we extract the letter before, after, below or above:

- ❖ **Boreas**   extract the letter above (North as a compass point)
- ❖ **Notus**   extract the letter below (South as a compass point)
- ❖ **Zephyrus**   extract the letter before (West as a compass point)
- ❖ **Eurus**   extract the letter after (East as a compass point)

Going through the extract in order, we take out letters as follows:

Eurus **W**	Zephyrus **H**	Eurus **I**	Zephyrus **S**	Eurus **T**
Notus **L**	Zephyrus **E**	Boreas **D**	Notus **O**	Eurus **W**
Zephyrus **N**	Boreas **T**	Zephyrus **H**	Notus **E**	Eurus **W**
Boreas **I**	Zephyrus **N**	Notus **D**		

The letters spell out:

'whistle down the wind'

which also fits the theme, the title and was why Homer Harvey told Andromeda that the solution had been 'a breeze'!

Teaching hint

> The key role for the teacher is to facilitate the work so that the pupils have to work hard at the solution without getting too frustrated. Able children should struggle to some extent and it would be wrong to give too much help before they have worked at the solution. Indeed, that would destroy the point of trying to make work challenging. On the other hand, frustration beyond a reasonable level can be damaging. The teacher should try to play as small a part as possible but when progress has stopped, the teacher should tease out clues and hints with the children rather than just giving the solution away too easily. This is a delicate judgement and demonstrates a key issue when working with able children.

Theme Nine: *Humanities*

Subject areas differ in terms of suitability of forms of differentiation. Humanities or social subjects (in Scottish terms) are unlikely to benefit from acceleration or differentiation by pace in the sense that you encourage children to go units, weeks or months ahead of others on the same course material. That is not to say that able pupils will not work at a greater pace and cover more work in a given time. Differentiation by resource is a favoured technique, as pupils working on the same topic in history or geography can use texts of differing complexities and levels of language. Differentiation by content is very possible as able pupils explore related areas by moving 'sideways' from the main theme. As much work can be set to elicit individual responses, differentiation by outcome is an obvious vehicle.

In relation to hierarchies of thinking skills, subjects such as history, geography, religious education, politics and philosophy have great capacity to develop analysis of evidence, interpretation, hypothesising, evaluation, sequencing, information-processing, problem-solving, decision-making, etc. There is a rich vein here to exploit. All of the subjects have vocabularies specific to them and which, again, provide material especially suitable for able pupils.

Decision Makers (page 184) plays to many of the thinking skills described above. It has a strong ethical and moral element. Empathy is an important feature, as is the realisation that difficult situations do not have an obvious answer or one upon which people can agree.

One of the difficulties of writing material in humanities for able children is that linking the work too closely to content can limit the use of the resources. *Decision Makers* has a more general context, which is transferable. *Eyam* (page 187) does relate to a particular situation at a given time, and indeed it is a very interesting situation. The skills of interpretation, analysis and evaluation apply more generally than just to this particular piece, and the work is best done before the pupils 'know too much'. This means that children are working at their own personal 'frontier of knowledge', so you get their own thinking and not regurgitation of other people's views.

On the Map (page 190) builds upon the work already required by the Scottish 5-14 Guidelines and the National Curriculum. A series of mapping skills is coupled with use of geographical vocabulary. Pupils have to follow some instructions precisely, and *On the Map* is a demanding piece of work. It also has open-ended features where individual children can show a greater degree of sophistication in their work, thus allowing differentiation by outcome.

This Theme is not very lengthy in itself but it should be seen in conjunction with other material. In the author's *'Effective Provision for Able and Talented Children'*, the activity called *What If* contains situations involving the social subjects, and *The Geography Person* combines human biology, geography and word play.

Elsewhere in this book there are relevant materials. For example, *DEPICT* (page 67) and *Quintessential Qualities* (page 71) in Theme Two: **Language Across the Curriculum** are appropriate, as are *The Question Is - History*, *The Question Is - Geography*, *Who Am I?* and *Just Imagine* (pages 223, 224, 228 and 235), all in Theme Eleven: **Alternative Answers, Imagination, Creativity**. In addition, Theme Ten: **Detective work** is of relevance, especially to historians, since analysis of evidence is such a key element in humanities.

DECISION MAKERS

Everybody has to make decisions. Some of them are more difficult than others. There are occasions when decisions can have far-reaching consequences. Look at the two situations described below and *make your decision*.

Situation one: **The wisdom of Solomon**

You may very well know about King Solomon, who was famous for making wise decisions. This is one of the problems that he had to face.

The Story

Two women came to Solomon, with a baby. Both women claimed to be the mother of the baby. Solomon was asked to make a decision. He said that he could not decide which was the true mother. He ordered for a sword to be brought so that the baby could be divided between them.

One woman agreed to this, saying that it was the fairest thing to do, but the second woman was horrified and said that she would rather see the baby go to the other woman. Solomon then ordered that the baby should go to the woman prepared to give up the child rather than see it harmed.

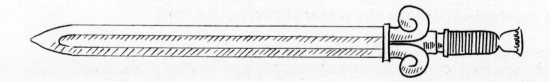

Your tasks

- Do you think that Solomon's decision was a wise one? Explain your answer.

- Put yourself in Solomon's place. How would you have come to a decision? (Do not use Solomon's own judgement and do not use methods not available so long ago in the past.)

- How could you resolve the problem quite easily in the present day?

DECISION MAKERS

Situation two: Life and death

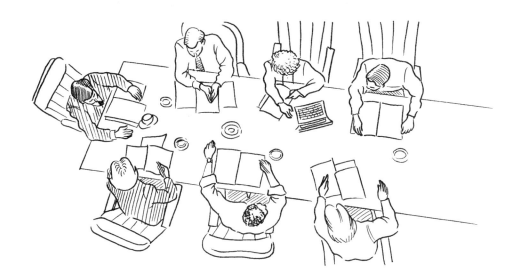

You are the Prime Minister of Glendia. The year is 1938, and you are at war with Marbary. The Marbars have been using a code for military instructions, which your own intelligence service has been trying to break. You have just been called away from a cabinet meeting to be given the message that the code has been broken. The Head of Intelligence has worked out that the Marbar airforce are going to launch a major air raid on the Glendian city of Downbridge tonight.

You are extremely pleased with the news and you have congratulated your intelligence service. However, you have an agonising decision to make. Your first reaction is to take special precautions to protect Downbridge and prevent serious damage and loss of life. The Head of Intelligence explains, though, that such action would probably convince the Marbar government that their code had been broken. As a result the code would be withdrawn and a new one substituted in its place, and consequently knowledge of the enemy's future plans would be lost.

Shortly you will return to your cabinet colleagues with your decision. They will want to hear your reasons in detail - especially Mr Leggon who is MP for Downbridge. Think carefully - it is a matter of life and death!

Your task

Write the notes that you are going to use in the cabinet meeting. They should contain the possible lines of action, your decision, the plans that you are putting into operation and the detailed arguments you will use to convince your colleagues.

DECISION MAKERS

Teaching notes

Problem-solving and decision-making are important skills for all children and they open up additional lines of thought where able pupils are concerned. There is no set answer so that individual responses will be very different in a number of ways, including the level of sophistication. As a result, differentiation by outcome will take place.

Key elements

There are a number of elements involved including:

- ❖ analysis of the situation
- ❖ a sense of time - the solutions must fit the past
- ❖ problem-solving
- ❖ hypothesising about the outcomes of different lines of action
- ❖ empathy
- ❖ decision-making
- ❖ evaluation of the consequences of decisions
- ❖ persuasive argument
- ❖ the realisation that some decisions do not have a 'right answer'

The wisdom of Solomon

Most children will see the wisdom in Solomon's judgement. It will be interesting to see what other solutions they can find. In the present day it would be a simple matter to carry out DNA tests.

Life and death

This is the sort of situation faced by Winston Churchill during the Second World War. The codebreakers at Bletchley Park cracked the German Enigma coding machine, but taking advantage of the knowledge gained had to be weighed against the possibility that the Germans would realise that the code had been broken and would then use another system.

The ethical and moral implications of 'Life and death' are very challenging. Persuading others of the correctness of the decision is a demanding task.

EYAM

In 1665, the fever known as the Great Plague came to London. In May, 43 people died of the disease; in September 30,000 died.

The Derbyshire village of Eyam had its first case in September 1665. The victim was a tailor called George Vicars who stayed with the Cooper family in a cottage close to the church. He, and all the Cooper family, died and the only person of the household to survive was Mrs Vicars.

The plague continued to spread in the village. By May 1666, there had been 77 deaths. In June 1666, the number of deaths rose sharply, 19 being recorded. In July there were 56 deaths and August was the worst month of all with no fewer than 77 dead. There was then a sudden decrease and October was the last month in which plague deaths were recorded.
The original population of Eyam before the outbreak had been approximately 1000. At the start of the trouble the number dropped to 350. Of these 350, only 83 remained alive by late October 1666.

Your tasks

✍ Plague was carried by black rats and fleas. When a rat died the fleas left its body. Sometimes they transferred to a human and passed on the plague while feeding on the person's blood. People in close contact with each other passed on the germs to one another.

How would you explain the outbreak of plague in Eyam, which was a considerable distance away from London?

✍ How is the following nursery rhyme connected to the plague?

> *Ring-a-ring-a-roses,*
> *A pocket full of posies,*
> *Atishoo - Atishoo,*
> *We all fall down.*

✍ In times of crisis somebody needs to take control. In Eyam the rector, William Mompesson, took charge of the situation. Imagine yourself to be Mompesson. How would you have dealt with the problems in Eyam? You need to consider both the welfare of the people of Eyam and the need to protect the inhabitants of the neighbouring areas. Remember to use only methods that were available in the 1660s.

When you have made your own decisions look at the separate sheet, which details the actions taken by Mompesson. Compare your plan with his decisions. What do you think of the way that Mompesson dealt with the problem?

William Mompesson, Rector Of Eyam

At the start of the outbreak, Mompesson sent his children, George and Elizabeth, away. He tried to get his wife, Catherine, to leave but she refused to go.

Mompesson called the whole village together and persuaded them to stay inside an imaginary circle a mile in diameter around the village and so prevent the disease from spreading to the rest of Derbyshire. He made an arrangement with the Duke of Devonshire to keep the village supplied. Provisions and medical supplies were left near what became known as Mompesson's Well. Mompesson left money in the water, which was sprinkled with vinegar to avoid spreading the disease. Letters to the Duke informed him about the number of deaths and how the villagers were coping.

At the height of the outbreak Mompesson stopped holding his services in the church for fear that they would increase the risk of infection. He felt, however, that the surviving villagers did need support and contact. His solution was to hold his services outside in a little dale close by called 'The Delf' or 'Cucklet Dell'. The villagers could stand well away from each other and yet were all able to hear Mompesson as the sound travelled well from the 'Pulpit Rock' on which he stood.

In August 1666, Mompesson suffered a personal tragedy when his wife, Catherine, fell victim to the plague and died. His personal leadership has been highly regarded. Even at the end of the outbreak it was Mompesson who set an example by burning his clothes himself.

EYAM

Teaching notes

Eyam has its own content but the subject matter is not the key feature. Even so, the story of Eyam is interesting. A visit to the village is very worthwhile to see the church, the plague cottages, the Riley graves, Mompesson's Well and the Cucklet Dell.

The piece promotes use of the higher-order thinking skills that are so important for able pupils. The work can be used for all the class or group, but individual responses result in differentiation by outcome.

Key elements

Eyam involves a number of elements including:

- ❖ interpretation of evidence
- ❖ a second layer of meaning in the nursery rhyme
- ❖ analysis of the situation facing the villagers
- ❖ problem-solving and decision-making
- ❖ empathy through putting oneself in Mompesson's shoes
- ❖ evaluation in judging Mompesson's actions

The work is tackled best before the children have too much prior knowledge. This means that they are thinking for themselves.

The tasks

- ❖ The outbreak in Eyam is normally attributed to a parcel of cloth, which was sent to George Vicars from London. The cloth was damp so Vicars dried it in front of the fire. One view is that this released plague vapours into the air. A second is that fleas were carried in the cloth and the warmth made them active. The pupils may come up with a number of acceptable suggestions.

- ❖ The 'ring of roses' refers to the marks caused by the plague. The 'pocket full of posies' was a container of herbs that was used to try to ward off the disease. 'Atishoo, Atishoo' is symbolic of the sneezing and fever. Death nearly always resulted, thus 'we all fall down'.

- ❖ The pupils may devise plans similar to those actually used by Mompesson. They may find his decision to send away his own children dubious in view of his appeal to the villagers.

Extension work

1 The outbreak could be considered in the context of the state of medicine and public hygiene at that time. The pupils could consider how an outbreak would be handled today. Both television and the cinema have used this theme.

2 Many of the figures used for the numbers of inhabitants and deaths are approximations. It would be useful to discuss the problem of historians in dealing with population statistics.

ON THE MAP

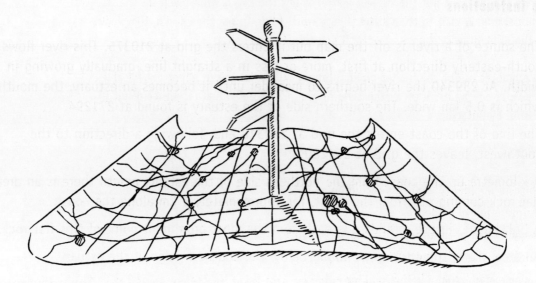

Whether in a local town, up the Amazon, in the middle of London or out in the wilds of the Scottish Highlands, you can always find out where you are and what direction to follow when you have the area 'on the map'. Now let us reverse the position so that you, yourself, construct the map for an area, using Ordnance Survey symbols, a scale and geographical terms.

Your task

Use the blank sheet, marked out in squares, to create a map by following the instructions below. On some occasions, positions and features will be exact, but at other times there is some choice in what you include and where you place it.

General instructions

1 Work with an actual map or book that contains Ordnance Survey symbols and use those symbols on your map.

2 Follow six-figure grid references by using the numbers on the blank sheet.

3 The scale is such that one side of each individual square represents 1 km.

4 The specific instructions guide you in putting features on the grid but without names - you add names that seem to be appropriate to you.

5 Enter features in pencil first, until you are sure of positions from later instructions; then use appropriate colours as per Ordnance Survey symbols.

ON THE MAP

Specific instructions

1. The source of a river is off the map but it enters the grid at 210375. This river flows in a south-easterly direction at first, more or less in a straight line, gradually growing in width. At 239340 the river begins to meander until it becomes an estuary, the mouth of which is 0.5 km wide. The southern side of the estuary is found at 271294.

2. The line of the coast enters the grid at 290318 and, following a direction to the southwest, leaves the grid at 264280.

3. A kilometre up the coast from the northern side of the estuary mouth there is an area of flat rock coming out from the coast, for approximately 1 km along the coast.

4. A lighthouse, in use, stands due east from the most prominent point of this flat rock.

5. An area of marshland is to be found below the southern edge of the estuary.

6. A tributary of the river rises at 255365 and joins the river at 236344. This tributary passes through an area of coniferous woodland, the size of which is 4 km^2.

7. A railway line enters the grid at 210378. It follows a route close to the northern bank of the river, passing over the tributary by means of a bridge. From the point where the river begins to meander, the railway follows as straight a line as possible, going through a cutting in a small hill for 1 km to reach the station at the mouth of the estuary.

8. To the west of the estuary is an area of natural beauty, including a non-coniferous wood of some 8 km^2. On the eastern edge of this woodland there is a Youth Hostel and due south of the hostel there is a picnic site. The area is served by a secondary road, which enters the grid at 210347 and exits at 222280.

9. The railway station serves a town on the side of the estuary. The town is served by a main road coming from the north, skirting the area of coniferous woodland, which then leaves the town in a north-easterly direction. Among the features of the town are a tourist information centre, two churches (one with a tower, one with a spire) and a Post Office.

10. A golf course is to be found north of the town, beside the main road. There was some difficulty in siting this course due to National Trust property and two sites of historical interest in the vicinity.

Extension

Having followed the instructions, you will have a map of important features. Some points are fixed while others are open to interpretation. You can now make your map more sophisticated by adding in appropriate details such as other roads, additional public facilities, buildings and natural features.

ON THE MAP

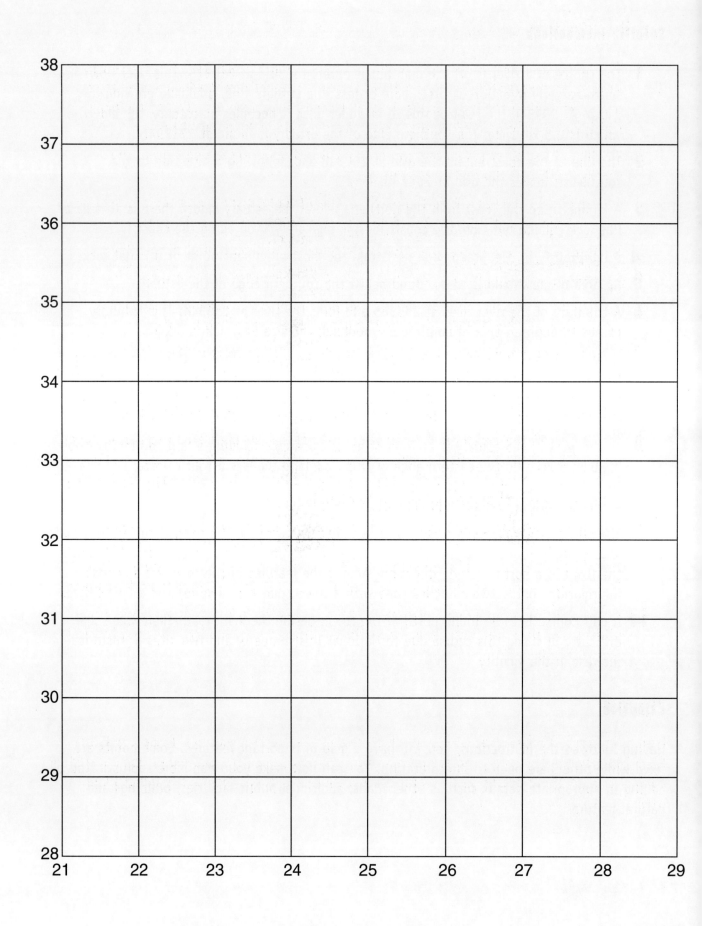

Effective Resources for Able and Talented Children © Barry Teare (Network Educational Press, 1999)

ON THE MAP

Teaching notes

Making and using maps figures in curriculum guidelines for England and Scotland. This activity allows pupils to make their own maps using specific instructions.

Some features to be drawn on the grid have exact locations; many can be interpreted in a number of ways, thus allowing individuality of response. Allowing pupils to add their own information to produce a more sophisticated and therefore realistic map can enhance differentiation by outcome. The 'solution' sheet that follows shows *one possible* answer containing the essential elements plus an interpretation where there is scope for different responses. Good answers can vary considerably. For technical reasons, this 'solution' is in black and white whereas pupils should have used appropriate colours - brown for contour lines, blue for rivers, red for youth hostel, and so on.

Key elements

On the Map is a demanding piece of work involving:

❖ following instructions precisely

❖ cross-referencing data

❖ understanding geographical vocabulary

❖ organisational skills

❖ using Ordnance Survey symbols

❖ using six-figure grid references

❖ working to scale

❖ following directions using the points of the compass

❖ creativity and imagination for the extension work

This exercise is therefore very suitable for able pupils, especially as so much is attempted at the same time.

Contexts

On the Map can be used in various ways:

❖ as extension work for able pupils where more standard tasks on maps have been completed

❖ as part of an enrichment session

❖ as an open-access competition

❖ as differentiated homework

Criteria

The quality of the responses will be judged on criteria including:

- ❖ features placed exactly, when required to do so
- ❖ sensible interpretation where variations are possible
- ❖ accuracy in using Ordnance Survey symbols, including colour
- ❖ the appropriateness of names given to features e.g. Delmouth at the estuary of the River Del
- ❖ interpretation and correct application of geographical terms e.g. meander
- ❖ correct use of scale
- ❖ the appropriateness of additional features if the extension work is undertaken

The teacher should advise the use of pencil at first, as later instructions may change a feature already included.

Effective Resources for Able and Talented Children © Barry Teare (Network Educational Press, 1999)

ON THE MAP

Solution

This grid shows the main features that should be included in the map, and represents one possible 'solution' to the activity.

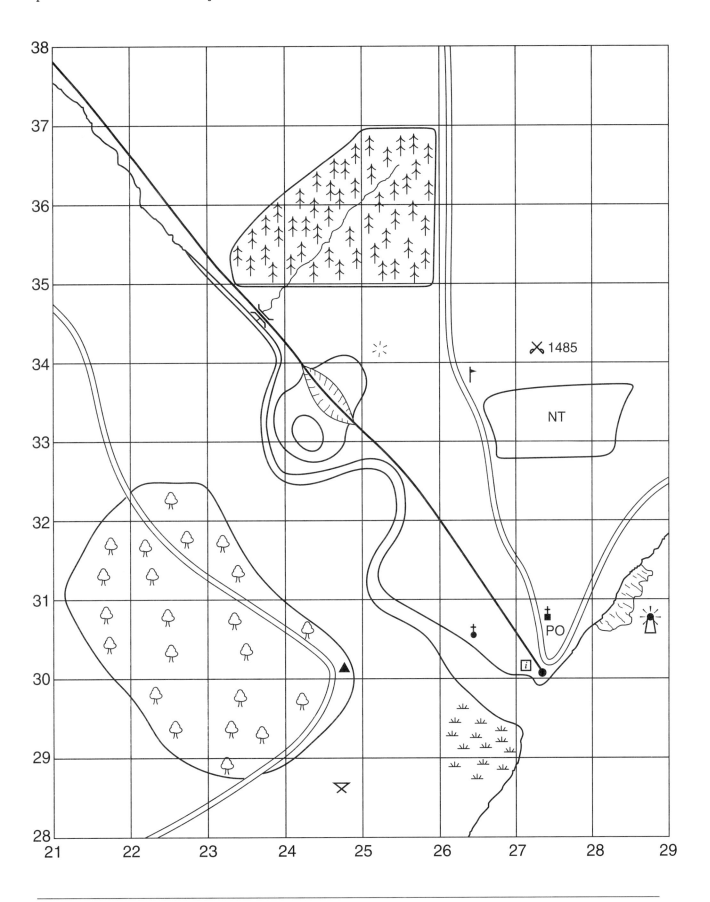

Effective Resources for Able and Talented Children © Barry Teare (Network Educational Press, 1999)

Theme Ten: *Detective Work*

A good proportion of the population, both adults and children, is fascinated by detective work. Detective fiction is a flourishing genre and detective series are very popular on television and the radio. It is interesting that well accepted writers of the modern era include leading crime writers such as P. D. James and Ruth Rendell. They are regarded as good writers who happen to centre their books on crime, in the same way that Len Deighton and John le Carré, whose genre is the thriller, are held in esteem. Able children are not only interested in detective work but they benefit greatly from practising the skills involved.

One of the great challenges to teachers is to deliver content and practice in the thinking skills in a challenging and entertaining manner. The content of detective work has important links with the National Curriculum. In science, AT1 'Experimental and Investigative Science' concerns itself with observation, prediction, evidence and conclusions, among other things. The BNFL/ Royal Microscopical Society materials entitled *'The Young Detectives'* deal with a 'whodunnit' en route to a more general consideration of:

- planning experimental work
- obtaining evidence
- considering evidence

The use of evidence, and its limitations, is central to history and geography. Many people regard history as detective work of the past. A fascinating area to explore is the history of crime detection itself, setting the crimes against the society of the day and the methods available to the police.

In English, the detective novel is one of many genres to know and use. All the Key Stages for English in the National Curriculum require children to consider the characteristics of different kinds of writing: argument, reports, commentary and explanations can be used in detective work.

Genre features strongly in the Scottish 5-14 Guidelines for English Language. The information for Level E, Writing, talks of the:

> *... skills of selecting facts, grouping information, emphasizing key ideas, manipulating materials from more than one source...*

Detective materials can certainly provide opportunities for practising these skills. The science guidelines require pupils to make and test hypotheses, and to make judgements about what evidence is relevant and reliable. Similar references are to be found at Level E for the social subjects and for technology.

Seeing is Believing (page 199) challenges our thoughts about first-hand knowledge, while showing how little we know from that source. It encourages healthy scepticism through a series of experiments and follow-ups. The material does not contain pupil resources but is rather guidance to teachers on practical activities.

According to the Evidence (page 203) contains a good deal of data. The culprit is not difficult to spot but what is important is that children keep going until they have extracted *all* the relevant points. This is good practice for examination situations where a candidate can write sensible responses but still score poorly because he or she has not included anywhere near all the available information. Thinking skills of analysis, synthesis, deduction, inference and information processing are prominent.

An Arresting Problem (page 211) is a shorter, lighter piece but it plays to the same skills. Logical thought is at the centre of the work.

Vital Evidence (page 213) consists of a series of cases, each with one or two key issues, encouraging pupils to cut through to the core ingredient. This directness is a valuable skill to develop, especially in these days of 'information unlimited'.

Effective Resources for Able and Talented Children © Barry Teare (Network Educational Press, 1999)

SEEING IS BELIEVING

Teaching notes

There are no pupil sheets for *Seeing is Believing* because the exercise is based upon the teacher's delivery of one or more lessons, or upon use within an enrichment activity.

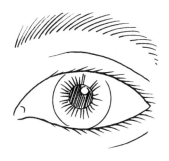

The work concerns the nature of evidence and whether or not it is better to see an event for yourself. Much of the work relates to eye-witnesses and the differences in what they believe that they have seen. The experiments and discussions involve children of all abilities but able pupils are likely to be more perceptive in the later stages when bias and conflicting statements are involved.

One simple experiment illustrates the need for information other than what we see ourselves.

Experiment 1

> CHOOSE A COUNTRY SUCH AS AUSTRALIA. GIVE THE PUPILS CLUES TO HELP IDENTIFY THIS COUNTRY, AND ASK THEM TO PUT THEIR HANDS UP WHEN THEY HAVE DONE SO. THE CLUES SHOULD BE DIFFICULT AT FIRST BUT THEY BECOME EASIER UNTIL THE FINAL CLUE SAYS, FOR EXAMPLE, THAT ONE OF THE MOST FAMOUS ANIMALS FROM THIS COUNTRY IS THE KANGAROO. BY THIS TIME EVERY CHILD, OR VIRTUALLY EVERY CHILD, KNOWS THE ANSWER -ASK ONE OF THEM TO NAME THE COUNTRY. THEN ASK FOR ALL THOSE WHO HAVE VISITED AUSTRALIA TO PUT UP THEIR HANDS. ONLY A SMALL NUMBER WILL DO SO.

Follow-up

A discussion follows this experiment, to explore its meaning. What becomes clear is that very little of our knowledge comes from first-hand experience. The class can then list:

❖ what they have seen for themselves
❖ the sources of the bulk of their knowledge

This leads naturally into a discussion of the problems associated with knowledge from other people, especially the problem of bias.

The next stage is to examine the hypothesis that seeing is believing. The story of Doubting Thomas in the Bible could be introduced. The second experiment described next could be used, provided that a road is visible from the classroom or that the class can easily reach a road.

Experiment 2

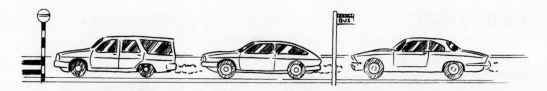

> ASK THE PUPILS TO WATCH THE ROAD UNTIL A CAR GOES BY. THEN ASK EACH
> CHILD IN TURN TO ESTIMATE THE CAR'S SPEED. THE ANSWERS NORMALLY VARY
> CONSIDERABLY, SHOWING THAT SEEING DOES NOT BRING AGREEMENT.

Follow-up

Discussion follows on why there are differences in people's accounts of the same event, on why some witnesses are more reliable than others, and why such evidence could be important (if an accident had taken place on the road, for instance). The notion of varying degrees of expertise enters the equation. Drivers are more likely to be accurate estimators of speed than non-drivers.

Experiment 3

> ASK SOMEBODY TO ENTER THE CLASSROOM AT A PRE-ARRANGED TIME IN THE
> LESSON, TALK BRIEFLY TO YOU AND LEAVE. THE PUPILS SHOULD NOT BE MADE
> AWARE THAT THIS IS GOING TO HAPPEN, NOR THAT THE EVENT WILL BE
> DISCUSSED. THEN ASK THEM TO WRITE A DETAILED DESCRIPTION OF THE PERSON
> WHO ENTERED THE ROOM AND TO RECORD WHAT WAS SAID. COMPARE THE
> ACCOUNTS AND NOTE THE DIFFERENCES.

Follow-up

Discussion can include circumstances in which such descriptions would be important - from witnesses to a crime, to provide 'identikit' pictures, etc. How well could the pupils see? Did some have a restricted view? Why is it that some people give statements with detailed accounts even though they could not see? (Perhaps they don't want to miss their 'big moment', they are attention-seeking, or find the attention flattering to egos.)

Experiment 4

> A VARIATION ON THIS EXPERIMENT IS TO HAVE THREE OR FOUR PEOPLE ENACT A
> SCENE IN FRONT OF THE CLASS WITHOUT THE CLASS REALISING THAT IT IS
> GOING TO HAPPEN. THE PUPILS' ACCOUNTS NOW ARE DESCRIPTIONS OF WHAT
> THEY SAW.

Follow-up

Again the differences in pupils' accounts are noted. The same influences as above are relevant but now the activity that has taken place is more complicated. As a result, the accounts are less likely to be accurate in terms of detail and chronology, and different

Effective Resources for Able and Talented Children © Barry Teare (Network Educational Press, 1999)

interpretations of the moods and motives of the people involved in the 'scene' also come into play. The importance of establishing the order of events can be discussed, particularly in connection with cases of assault, when knowing who acted first is likely to be vital.

Experiment 5

THE EXPERIMENTS USED SO FAR HAVE SHOWN THAT FIRST-HAND EVIDENCE HAS MANY PROBLEMS EVEN WHEN WITNESSES ARE TRYING TO TELL THE TRUTH AS THEY SEE IT. NOW THE QUESTION OF BIASED WITNESSES IS INTRODUCED. A SPORTING EVENT SUCH AS A FOOTBALL MATCH PROVIDES A GOOD EXAMPLE. MANY PEOPLE SEE THE SAME EVENTS BUT HAVE A DIFFERENT VIEW OF WHAT THEY HAVE SEEN. PERHAPS A PARTICULAR EVENT COULD BE USED HERE.

Follow-up

Discussion follows on other situations where doubt may be expressed about the views of witnesses. For example, a general of an army involved in a war might see what he wants to see, while other witnesses involved might see things entirely differently.

Experiment 6

OBSERVATION IS VERY IMPORTANT IN THE CONTEXT OF THE WORK UNDER DISCUSSION. TAKE THE CLASS ON A PRE-PREPARED WALK AROUND AN AREA CLOSE TO THE SCHOOL. DECIDE BEFOREHAND WHAT OBJECTS AND EVENTS YOU WANT PUPILS TO OBSERVE.

Follow-up

Following the walk, pupils should be questioned regarding what has been observed, either verbally or in written form. The observations may involve shapes, colours, numbers, written notices - the greater the variety the better. Children work individually, in pairs or small groups. The accuracy of their observations is tested. This could be done in a competitive team manner if the teacher so wished.

Conclusion

The various experiments and follow-ups can be drawn together to examine:

- ❖ the advantages of first-hand knowledge
- ❖ the limitations as to the extent of first-hand knowledge
- ❖ the differences between eye-witness accounts, and the reasons for them
- ❖ the flaws in the argument that 'seeing is believing'

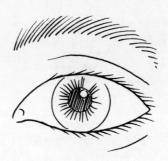

ACCORDING TO THE EVIDENCE

In the early hours of one Sunday morning Inspector Hawthorn was summoned to Laburnum Grange. The owner, Mr Beech, had been shot dead in his home and a murder investigation began. The inspector and his colleagues made a thorough search and the police surgeon, Doctor Ash, examined the body and later gave instructions for tests to be carried out in the laboratory.

Questions

Read the information provided on the following sheets and then answer these questions.

1 Give six reasons why Inspector Hawthorn quickly came to the conclusion that the murder had been carried out by somebody staying in the house, rather than by an intruder.

2 What led the police immediately to the belief that Mr Beech had been shot with the revolver? Explain the test they could use in the laboratory to prove that this was the murder weapon.

3 Fingerprints did not provide useful evidence in this case. Explain why you think that was so.

4 A torn piece of paper was found on the floor. An incomplete message was left. Write down what you think the full message said.

5 After a thorough investigation and careful examination of the evidence, Inspector Hawthorn arrested Mr Elm for the murder of Mr Beech. In a talk with his colleagues Inspector Hawthorn listed 10 reasons why he suspected Mr Elm. See if you can write down what these reasons were.

6 Assuming that Mr Elm had been justly accused, you are asked to give an explanation of why he committed the crime. Give as much detail as possible. There are various possibilities that you could use but try not to suggest an idea that does not fit the facts or is not *'according to the evidence'*.

ACCORDING TO THE EVIDENCE

A: The house, Laburnum Grange

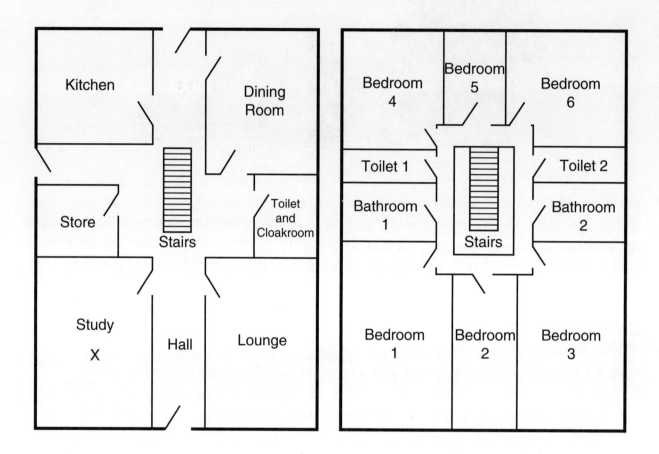

The body was found at the place marked X in the study. Upstairs Mr and Mrs Beech were in their normal bedroom (1). Bedroom 2 was the one that had been used by their son Gerald Beech before he married and left home. The son's passion for loud pop music had led Mr Beech to have sound-proofing installed in Gerald's room to prevent the noise carrying. Gerald had always joked that the sound-proofing had kept his parents' noise out so that he was not disturbed! During the weekend of the tragedy bedroom 2 was occupied by Mr Elm. The other large bedroom (3) was used by Mr and Mrs Pine, and bedrooms 4 and 5 were taken by Mr Yew and Mrs Larch respectively. Bedroom 6 was unoccupied on the night of the tragedy.

ACCORDING TO THE EVIDENCE

B: The people

MR AND MRS BEECH

Mr and Mrs Beech are the owners of the house, and the hosts. They had invited a number of guests for a relaxing weekend. Mr Beech is a successful businessman who manages a firm of shoe manufacturers.

MR ELM

Mr Elm has known Mr Beech for a long time as a business associate rather than as a friend. Mr Elm has become a partner in Mr Beech's business. He had first met Mr Beech through playing cricket in a local league and in his youth Mr Elm had been a good left-arm bowler and batsman.

MR AND MRS PINE

Mr and Mrs Pine are long-standing friends of the Beech family. Indeed Mr Pine had been Best Man at the Beechs' wedding.

MISS OAK

Miss Oak knows Mr and Mrs Beech because she was a neighbour of theirs at a previous house. Arthritis in her legs makes movement up stairs difficult.

MR YEW

Mr Yew attended the same school as Mr Beech and the friendship has been maintained ever since.

MRS LARCH

Mrs Larch has been invited for the weekend because of her close links with Mrs Beech at the local church.

ACCORDING TO THE EVIDENCE

C: The events

This is a description of the events leading up to the tragedy, put together as a result of police interviews.

The guests had arrived at various times on the Friday evening. A cold meal was ready so that it could be eaten once everybody was assembled. After the meal a game of cards had been organised. On Saturday morning the whole party had intended to go out walking but the weather was very bad. It rained heavily throughout Saturday so that the guests stayed indoors. The one exception was Mr Elm who went to the mobile blood donor van to give a pint of his blood, joking that he hoped his habits of smoking cigars and drinking rum would not damage the product! He explained that his group (AB negative) was rare and therefore he did not want to miss the session despite the weather. He did, however, complain on his return that the van had been situated on an unmade car park and as a result his shoes had got very muddy.

In the evening Mr and Mrs Beech had organised party games in the study, which everybody thoroughly enjoyed. The gathering broke up at midnight and the guests retired to their own rooms. Mrs Beech went to bed but her husband stayed up saying that he 'had some business to attend to' and he seemed a little upset. Mr Beech would not say anything further but his wife knew that financial problems at work had been bothering him for some time and she gathered that he was particularly concerned about some figures that would be presented to the tax inspectors shortly.

At one o'clock in the morning pandemonium broke out. A loud bang was heard and then there were sounds of voices and people moving. Miss Oak was sleeping in a temporary bed in the lounge because of her problem in climbing stairs. Despite her incapacity she could move fairly well on the level and she was quickly out of her room to see what was happening. She met Mr Elm who was clearly in a very excited condition. He explained that in his room he had heard what sounded like a shot and had come downstairs to see what had caused the noise. Soon afterwards the other guests and Mrs Beech arrived at the entrance to the study.

ACCORDING TO THE EVIDENCE

D: The scene of the crime

Police searching the garden and grounds found nothing of significance. The soil was very wet because of the heavy rain but there were no footprints to be found. All doors and windows were examined but they were all still securely fastened and nowhere was there any indication of an entry being forced. Three dogs - family pets - had their kennels to the side of the house near the study. They had not barked until one o'clock when the shot went off. They were naturally upset and had added to the general confusion by their barking.

2
and therefore you must rea
that your partner has be
falsifying the records and cheat
you and the company. Y
will have to discuss th
quickly with Mr E

Inside the study the police carried out a detailed investigation. A chair had been knocked over and there were other signs of a disturbance. The dead body of Mr Beech was lying on the floor. On the table nearby there were two glasses containing half-finished drinks. The glass closest to the chair next to Mr Beech's body contained whisky and the other glass had rum and blackcurrant in it. Near to another chair facing that presumably used by Mr Beech, the detectives found lumps of dried mud. The distinctive smell of a recently-smoked cigar hung in the air. A scrap of paper lay on the rug. It had been torn so that it looked as shown.

One of the drawers of the desk was open. Mrs Beech explained that her husband kept a loaded revolver in there since a spate of burglaries had started in the area, despite the fact that he should not have such a weapon in his possession. He had in fact shown his guests the weapon earlier that evening. The revolver was no longer in the drawer but it was soon found on the floor behind another piece of furniture. It smelt strongly and had obviously been recently fired. No fingerprints were found on the handle and it had obviously been rubbed clean. The rest of the room rendered many sets of prints but they were those of Mr and Mrs Beech and their guests.

E: Doctor Ash's report

Mr Beech had a cut and bruising on the right side of his face, which had bled. From the nature of the blow the attacker clearly had used considerable force. It also seemed very likely that the attacker was left-handed. Death, however, had been caused by a single shot fired from close range into the chest of the dead man. Analysis showed that Mr Beech's blood group was O positive and marks of this type were found on the carpet. During the interviews it was discovered that Mr Elm had a blood stain on his shirt. He explained that he had cut himself whilst shaving earlier. The laboratory reported that the stain on Mr Elm's shirt was of blood group O positive.

ACCORDING TO THE EVIDENCE

Teaching notes

Pupils are required to sift through a variety of written evidence to reach their conclusions. They need to combine the different pieces. The work involves a number of skills including:

- ❖ information processing

- ❖ deduction and inference

- ❖ logical thinking

- ❖ analysis

- ❖ synthesis (bringing all the information together and making something out of it)

- ❖ a piece of writing taking account of the facts but allowing alternative explanations of the underlying motive

Some pupils ignore the weight of evidence and try to find outlandish solutions. It is worthwhile to discuss the idea of evidence 'beyond reasonable doubt'.

Contexts

The work could be carried out in a number of ways:

- ❖ as normal classwork, perhaps linked to evidence within the history syllabus

- ❖ as a discussion piece, in groups

- ❖ using written answers

- ❖ as differentiated homework

- ❖ as an extension piece from a forensic science unit

- ❖ as an 'unseen' to give practice in handling material without other preparation

- ❖ as part of a wider enrichment activity on detection, logical thought and deduction

Effective Resources for Able and Talented Children © Barry Teare (Network Educational Press, 1999)

Solutions

Question 1

Pupils were asked for six reasons why the murderer had almost certainly been staying in the house, but there are more than that to be found.

1 There were no footprints in the grounds even though the soil was wet after heavy rain.
2 There was no indication of a forced entry.
3 The dogs had not barked prior to the shot itself even though their kennels were close to the scene of the crime.
4 The room had recently been occupied by two people who had been drinking, which suggests that Mr Beech met one of his guests.
5 Mr Beech's revolver had been used and he had shown his guests the gun, and where it was positioned, earlier in the evening.
6 Cigar smoke in the air suggests that a recent meeting had taken place but not with an intruder.
7 Mr Beech had told his wife that he 'had some business to attend to' and this indicates a possible meeting.
8 The torn paper found in the room indicates a discussion with one of the guests about a financial problem. Already Mr Elm is implicated.
9 Fingerprints in the study were from Mr and Mrs Beech and their guests only.

Question 2

Death was clearly by shooting. The sound of the gun going off had woken up the household. The revolver was lying on the floor. It had recently been fired.

The test in the laboratory is the one point where outside knowledge is needed beyond the information in the sheets. The bullet in the body is recovered, cleaned and photographed in a magnified form. A second bullet is fired from the suspect gun into a blank target and again a magnified photograph is taken. If the gun fired both bullets the marks (striation marks) on the bullets will be identical because every gun produces different marks when it is fired, but every bullet fired by the same gun is marked in the same way.

Question 3

The revolver had been wiped clean so that no fingerprints were found. Elsewhere in the room the problem was the opposite - there were too many prints. All the guests had been at a party in that room earlier. Naturally their prints were all over the place but for innocent reasons.

Question 4

The message could read:

> 2
>
> and therefore you must realise
> that your partner has been
> falsifying the records and cheating
> you and the company. You
> will have to discuss the matter
> quickly with Mr Elm.

Credit should be given for other possible answers that fit the gaps and make sense.

Question 5

Ten reasons why Mr Elm was suspected of the murder were requested, but there are at least twelve.

1   The torn message contains the name of Mr Elm (probably).

2   Mr Beech was going to discuss a business matter, and Mr Elm is his partner.

3   Mr Beech was worried about a financial problem and the torn letter indicates that Mr Elm was cheating the company.

4   Mr Elm was first on the scene even though his room was the furthest away and he had to go right round the landing to reach the top of the stairs.

5   Mr Elm claimed that he heard a shot but he was in bedroom 2, which was sound-proofed.

6   Miss Oak found Mr Elm in an excited condition.

7   Mr Elm enjoys drinking rum and one of the half-finished glasses contained rum and blackcurrant.

8   A cigar had recently been smoked and we know that Mr Elm smokes cigars.

9   Lumps of dried mud were found on the floor. The most likely explanation is that they came off the bottom of Mr Elm's shoes because he had been to give blood in the afternoon and the blood donor vehicle was on an unmade car park where the ground was wet and muddy. The other guests had not left the house that day.

10   The attacker seems to have been a man from the force of the blow.

11   The attacker was probably left-handed and we know that Mr Elm had been a left-arm bowler and batsman.

12   Mr Elm had a blood stain on his shirt that he claimed was the result of a shaving accident. However, the blood was not his own group, AB negative, but rather 0 positive - the same as Mr Beech, the murdered man.

Question 6

There are a number of possible motives for the crime, but the children should make use of the available information, which is likely to link the crime to an argument over financial matters within the company.

Effective Resources for Able and Talented Children © Barry Teare (Network Educational Press, 1999)

AN ARRESTING PROBLEM

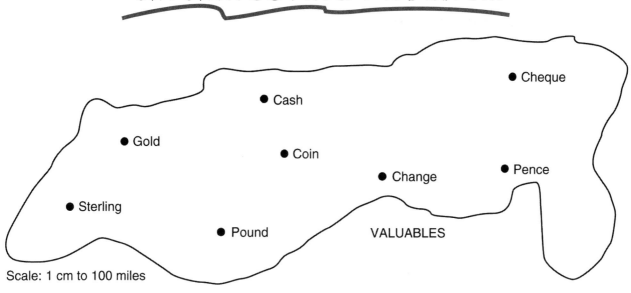

Scale: 1 cm to 100 miles

The police are investigating the theft of valuable jewellery from the home of millionaire Lord Moneymaker on the outskirts of the town of Sterling, in a country called Valuables.

The crime took place between 10 pm and midnight on Thursday June 4th. It involved the thief scaling a high wall and entering by a very small window, and the method used obviously involved considerable agility and strength. A servant caught sight of the thief as he was leaving but was unable to stop him. He was able to tell the police that the thief had black hair and it became obvious that the crime had been carried out by one man on his own.

The computer has identified 10 suspects whose past histories indicate that they are likely candidates: ADAM ALSATIAN, COLIN CORGI, FRANK FOXHOUND, BARRY BULLDOG, DAVID DALMATIAN, LARRY LABRADOR, PERCY POODLE, ROGER RETRIEVER, TIM TERRIER, WILLIAM WHIPPET.

Your task

Presuming that the crime was committed by one of the named suspects, whom would you arrest if you were in possession of the following information?

1   The guilty man's hobbies include gardening, photography and cards. The last activity has been somewhat restricted as his wife does not like playing cards.
2   Frank Foxhound was breathalysed near Change at 9 pm on the evening of June 4th.
3   The guilty man is a close friend of Adam Alsatian and Larry Labrador.
4   Tim Terrier's nickname is Ginger because of the colour of his hair.
5   Percy Poodle called at the Post Office in Gold at 4 pm on June 4th.
6   Adam Alsatian and Colin Corgi always work as a team.
7   Roger Retriever and David Dalmatian both had wedding anniversaries on May 26th. David celebrated his golden wedding which meant that he had been married for five times as long as Roger.
8   William Whippet and Barry Bulldog are known to their friends as 'Little and Large'. Barry, at 1.95 m and 105 kg, towers above his old friend William.
9   Larry Labrador and Roger Retriever share an interest in stamp collecting although they only met for the first time at a stamp fair a week before the theft under investigation.
10 Two suspects' wives, Winifred Whippet and Caroline Corgi, are Bridge partners.

AN ARRESTING PROBLEM

Teaching notes

This logical thought problem involves:

- ❖ information processing
- ❖ deduction and inference
- ❖ combining data to produce the necessary information
- ❖ the use of scale

The work can be linked to other aspects of detective material and evidence. The notion of having an alibi could be developed as an extension. Material of this sort fits alongside aspects of history and science amongst other curriculum areas. *An Arresting Problem* does not take very long to do and can be used as one of the many items on hand when children finish other work ahead of the majority of the class. The vehicle used is an entertaining one and the odd names of the suspects and of the places will appeal to the quirky sense of humour of many able children.

Solution

1 This clue does not tell us anything on its own.

2 Frank Foxhound is eliminated as he was over 800 miles away from the scene of the crime shortly before the crime took place.

3 Adam Alsatian and Larry Labrador are cleared.

4 Tim Terrier has red hair whereas the thief had black hair.

5 Percy Poodle was 200 miles or so from the scene of the crime between six and eight hours before the break-in. This is not conclusive and does not help the investigation.

6 Colin Corgi is eliminated, as the thief was on his own whereas Colin always works with Adam who has already been cleared.

7 David Dalmatian is approximately 70 years old and cannot be regarded as a likely candidate for such an 'athletic' crime. Roger Retriever could be very young and cannot be ignored.

8 Barry Bulldog could not have entered through a small window although William Whippet could have done so.

9 Roger Retriever has only recently met Larry Labrador whereas the guilty man is a close friend of Larry's (Clue **3**). Roger cannot be the thief of the jewels in this case.

10 We are down to two men only - Percy Poodle and William Whippet. William's wife plays cards whereas the guilty man's does not (Clue **1**).

This leaves you to arrest *Percy Poodle*.

VITAL EVIDENCE

In detective cases there are many factors to consider but often particular incidents or features provide vital evidence.

Case one: Eye spy

Mrs Wright was doing her round of the shops on Thursday March 9th as usual. First stop had been the Post Office to collect her pension. Then she called at the bread shop and bought a wholemeal loaf. Next she was going to visit the greengrocer's. Mrs Wright hoped that there would be some conference pears as good as the ones last week. She looked down at the shopping list and then shook her head. She could not read it. Her glasses had been damaged the day before and they were at the opticians for repair. Her long-sightedness was certainly a problem.

Just as Mrs Wright was about to cross the road she heard shouting. Some thirty metres away there was a commotion as three men raced from the bank and threw themselves into a waiting car, which drove off furiously away from the elderly shopper.

When the police arrived Mrs Wright was taken to the police station where she made a statement about what she had seen.

Your Task

When the police were preparing a case against the men who were arrested the next day after the bank raid, what reliability do you think that they could place on the eye-witness account of Mrs Wright?

Case two: Paper exercise

A man was found murdered. In his pocket were a comb, a black pen, car keys, £3.65 in coins, a brown-and-white handkerchief and a piece of paper with this written on it:

The detective squad failed to make headway in the first days of the investigation. Ann Lock returned to work after illness and rejoined the squad. She was able to move the case on. When asked by a colleague what factor had been important, she replied that it was that the message or symbols had been written on what was otherwise a blank sheet of paper.

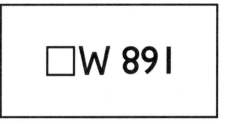

Your tasks

Decide what Ann Lock meant about the 'message' on the sheet of paper.

Give your interpretation of what the 'message' might mean.

VITAL EVIDENCE

Case three: A horse of a different colour

The most important race meeting of the year at Lancanton features the Spring Cup. It is a very valuable race and many trainers had prepared a horse especially for it.

On the day of the race an anonymous letter was received threatening that the race was going to be disrupted. The security team was alarmed at the possibility of the Spring Cup being ruined. They looked at the starting-stalls carefully and carried out a very detailed inspection of the course. Nothing was found. As the start of the race approached the security officers spread out across the racecourse to see if they could spot anything unusual.

At 3.32 pm the Spring Cup was run. Nothing untoward took place. The crowd was very happy to watch the favourite win by a length. Those holding winning tickets went to collect their money.

The security officers were baffled by the letter and the fact that nothing had happened to disrupt the race. They put it down to the action of a crank.

Later that day a valuable racehorse disappeared from the course without trace.

Your task

Members of the local CID were astonished when the Chief Constable asked them to work on both incidents and to give each equal attention. Can you work out why the Chief Constable made that particular request?

VITAL EVIDENCE

Case four: Turning the tables

During the investigation of the murder of a man in his twenties, the time of death was narrowed down to a very short period. He was seen alive by a friend at 8.20 am and by 8.45 am his body was discovered by the postwoman.

The detective squad began to question a number of people whom they felt might be implicated. Each was asked to give an account of his or her movements.

Tom was known to have long-standing bad relations with the murdered man. He explained to the police that on Friday June 1st he had rowed his boat from his home in the riverside village of Lacton down to the town of Lacmouth. He was seen leaving at 6.00 pm and friends where he was staying overnight confirmed his arrival to be 7.40 pm. On the following day, Saturday June 2nd his friends saw him row off back home at 7.15 am. Tom did not know his exact time of arrival back at Lacton but said that the evidence of the outward journey would place it at 8.55 am which puts him in the clear as far as the murder is concerned.

When Inspector Dark looked more closely into these times he made use of the following information:

1 The River Lac flows due south from its source past a number of villages including Lacton until it reaches the sea at the estuary town of Lacmouth.

2 On the days of June 1st and 2nd a very strong southerly wind was blowing in the area.

3 There had recently been a full moon and spring tides were taking place.

4 The tide times for the area on the critical days were:

Friday 1st	High Water Low Water	8.19 am and 8.44 pm 2.22 am and 2.49 pm
Saturday 2nd	High Water Low Water	9.03 am and 9.33 pm 3.03 am and 3.37 pm

Your task

Do you believe that Inspector Dark should accept Tom's story as being proof of his innocence?

VITAL EVIDENCE

Case five: On second thoughts

Jenny Davies was working undercover on the trail of a group thought to be responsible for large quantities of illegal drugs. She was carrying out her assignment in plain clothes.

On one particular morning she tracked the men to a café. She took a table some distance away from them so as not to draw attention to herself nor inhibit the conversation. This meant unfortunately that Jenny Davies could not hear their conversation very clearly. At times she could not hear at all. However, she was able to report back to her superior that a man had been mentioned by name - David Street, that she had heard the word 'key' and also some phrase about 'locking the ship at midnight on Friday'.

These pieces of information did not help the drug squad initially until they thought about alternative interpretations of the data.

Your task

Remembering that the undercover officer only heard snatches of the conversation, that she might have misheard and that she did not hear how the pieces fitted together, can you make sense of the information through other interpretations than that which Jenny Davies herself used?

VITAL EVIDENCE

Teaching notes

These days we are bombarded with information and data of all sorts. There is a real danger of information overload. As Michael Barber commented in 'The Learning Game' (Victor Gollanz, 1996), what we must not do is lose the power of reason in making sense of that information.

Vital Evidence involves a number of thinking skills, valued in curriculum guidelines in both England and Scotland, including:

- ❖ information processing
- ❖ word play
- ❖ hypothesising
- ❖ interpreting
- ❖ analysis
- ❖ deduction and inference
- ❖ finding alternative solutions

Contexts

The work could be used in a variety of ways:
- ❖ in total, during an extended time or enrichment activity
- ❖ as separate units
- ❖ for class discussion
- ❖ as individual written work
- ❖ as differentiated homework
- ❖ as a piece of enrichment material for able pupils finishing class-set tasks early and well

There follows some specific interpretations of the five cases. They are only suggested answers. Many, equally valid, suggestions may be put forward by children - indeed they should be encouraged to do so.

Case one: Eye spy

The fact that Mrs Wright is elderly (which we know because the adjective actually was used, and because she draws a pension) and that she has damaged her glasses, which are in for repair, could suggest that her evidence as an eye-witness might be questionable. However, she suffers from long-sightedness, which prevents her reading her shopping list without her glasses but does not impair her vision over reasonable distances. The defence counsel at the trial might find it difficult to discredit her evidence.

Case two: Paper exercise

The fact that the paper is otherwise blank means that we do not know which way up it was written. If we look at the message 'upside-down' it now looks like this:

This could lead to many different interpretations. One is that it is an address linked to the dead man, perhaps *'168 Manchester Square'*.

The children are likely to make a wide variety of suggestions. For example, it could represent the code to a lock or safe.

Case three: A horse of a different colour

The most likely explanation here is that the anonymous threat was sent by the same people who later kidnapped the horse. It was used as a diversion. The Chief Constable realised that the security guards would have had their attention on an earlier race. When that passed off without incident they would have relaxed and perhaps not have been concentrating upon their work in the later part of the afternoon. Thus both incidents are likely to be linked and the clues from the threat might help solve the disappearance of the horse.

Case four: Turning the tables

Tom's assertion that his first journey of 1 hour 40 minutes would be matched on the return journey needs close examination. If he had planned the crime carefully, he may well have wasted time on the outward leg so as to extend the length. Even if this is not the case, the times need close scrutiny by reference to the additional points considered by Inspector Dark. On the Friday evening Tom would be rowing against the tide. High water was not until 8.44 pm so that the tide was still coming up the river. On Saturday morning the tidal condition was the same - high water was not until 9.03 am. This time the tide was with him making it quicker to travel. A strong southerly wind was blowing both days i.e. from the sea, up the river. On Friday night Tom was rowing against this strong wind whereas on Saturday the wind was with him. At the time of spring tides the water levels are increased thus exaggerating the effect of the tide.

This data together suggests that the journey home would have been considerably quicker and easier. Was this enough to place Tom in the murder location at the critical time? The answer is probably yes but children might well suggest that interviews with local fishermen or the harbour master might allow more accurate interpretation.

Case five: On second thoughts

The important issues are that Jenny Davies could not hear properly or completely and that her pieces of information are out of context.

Children are likely to produce many different interpretations. So long as they fit the evidence, they are equally valid. One possibility is that 'David Street' refers to a place, not a man, that 'key' should be 'quay' and that 'locking' should be 'docking'. That interpretation would hang together. Many more are possible. The 'ship' might be a pub, for example.

Theme Eleven: *Alternative Answers, Imagination, Creativity*

Able children need space and challenge. They value the opportunity to develop an idea in an individual way. Closed questions are necessary to test knowledge and to check acquisition of facts. They do need, however, to be accompanied by open-ended situations and questions that encourage alternative answers or a variety of types of response. OFSTED has criticised 'over-directed teaching'. Able children revel in space.

These types of opportunities are linked with the areas of imagination and creativity. Once a situation is 'opened up', you are giving children the chance to use their imaginations and be creative in what they personally make of the work. The features go together very strongly. The outcomes are very varied and sometimes they are also surprising. Able children who are 'encouraged to fly' produce unexpected but brilliant responses, many of which cannot be predicted.

The original version of *The Question Is* is very open-ended and it has produced remarkable responses from both pupils and teachers over a number of years. The various items have been carefully compiled to promote different levels of complexity, which in turn is likely to determine the sophistication of the response. They give free rein to the imagination. Indeed, the teacher encourages the children to be creative in their thinking during the introduction to the work.

One of the key tasks for the teachers of able children is to present content in a challenging and enjoyable way. We are faced by set content in the National Curriculum, the Scottish 5-14 Guidelines and various examination courses. The danger is that we become so dominated by content that we fail to present it in a way that will appeal to able pupils.

The Question Is (page 221) is an example of open-ended material that encourages differentiation by outcome. The original content was general. This technique, like so many others, can be linked with any content. Three further versions of *The Question Is* are included to show application in science, history and geography. Other curriculum areas could be developed. The 'answers' could be restricted to particular sections of content within any course. They could act as an assessment assignment for able children at the end of a module or topic.

Or and *Who Am I?* (pages 226 and 228) give opportunities for alternative answers and for lateral thinking. They fit the humanities sections of the curriculum, or they can be included within thinking skills, perhaps even part of PSME - a very varied area looking to be expanded post-2000.

Now You See It (page 232) is included as a fun piece to stimulate the visual imagination. It promotes individuality of response and unusual interpretation. *Now You See It* can also be used as the stimulus for a piece of creative writing.

Just Imagine (page 235) combines analysis of the consequences of changes to our world and imaginative thinking about those changes. It is very much a cross-curricular piece. It can also be used to get children to create their own situations. Able children, in particular, are good at taking pieces of work on, making something more of them and taking more responsibility for their own learning programmes. This is an important form of differentiation and one supported in the Scottish 5-14 Guidelines.

Creativity and imagination are strong themes running through so many curriculum areas in the guidance for both the Scottish and English systems. English, science, technology, art and drama are among subjects where these elements have an important role to play. A limited number of items have been included in this theme, but pieces in many other themes have elements of imagination, creativity and alternative answers: for example, *The Bare Bones* (page 81), *Mole, Rat, Badger, Toad and ... Who?* (page 77), *Decision Makers* (page 184), *Quintessential Qualities* (page 71), *DEPICT* (page 67), *The Man in the Van* (page 96) and many others.

THE QUESTION IS

You are used to giving answers to questions set in a variety of ways. For some questions there is only one correct answer but on other occasions a number of responses are considered as being correct, even though some answers could be regarded as stronger than others. This exercise reverses the normal process by giving you the answer. Your task is to provide suitable questions. Try to give as many questions as possible to each of the answers that are listed. Look for both the obvious and the less obvious questions. These 'questions' could be in a simple written form or presented as a diagram, puzzle or problem.

The answers

1   blue
2   twenty seven
3   the third desk from the window on the row nearest to the door
4   July
5   they both weigh the same
6   3 hours 25 minutes
7

8   the oak tree
9   the guilty person was Robert
10 there would be two matches left
11 the Battle of Hastings
12 the person who finished third was Jane Williams
13 New York
14 it lives on both land and in water
15 10111
16 you would arrive at the bench
17 1980
18 the most direct route is George Street – Hall Road – Newtown Road – Denby Road
19 sister-in-law
20 south-east
21 **SEND HELP QUICKLY**
22 pathway C is the correct one
23 Napoleon Bonaparte
24 the odd one out is nylon
25 the Board of Inquiry decided that he was responsible for the disaster

---

THE QUESTION IS - SCIENCE

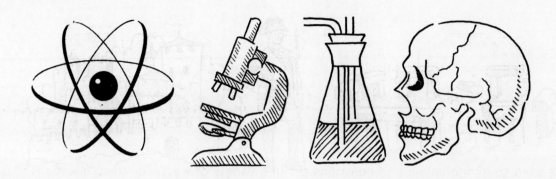

You are used to giving answers to questions set in a variety of ways. For some questions there is only one correct answer but on other occasions a number of responses are considered as being correct, even though some answers could be regarded as stronger than others. This exercise reverses the normal process by giving you the answer. Your task is to provide suitable questions. Try to give as many questions as possible to each of the answers that are listed. Look for both the obvious and the less obvious questions. These 'questions' could be in a simple written form or presented as a diagram, puzzle or problem.

The answers

1   myelin sheath

2   the Nobel prize in physics

3   it varies directly with the temperature

4   NH_4OH

5   a valency of 1

6   nimbostratus

7   pi bonds

8   a red-brown colour

9   a regular swinging motion

10   the A or Retinol group

11   Mohs' scale

12    $-269^{\circ}C$

13   15° of longitude

14   pH

15   friction

THE QUESTION IS - HISTORY

You are used to giving answers to questions set in a variety of ways. For some questions there is only one correct answer but on other occasions a number of responses are considered as being correct, even though some answers could be regarded as stronger than others. This exercise reverses the normal process by giving you the answer. Your task is to provide suitable questions. Try to give as many questions as possible to each of the answers that are listed. Look for both the obvious and the less obvious questions. These 'questions' could be in a simple written form or presented as a diagram, puzzle or problem.

The answers

1. an Act of Parliament
2. medieval
3. that he was an impostor
4. an anachronism
5. religious conflict
6. too little too late
7. nationalism
8. his grandson
9. the Schlieffen Plan
10. a giant step for women
11. Victorian values
12. complete reform was necessary
13. cholera
14. evacuation
15. crop rotation
16. conspiracy
17. only one of many causes
18. Waterloo

THE QUESTION IS - GEOGRAPHY

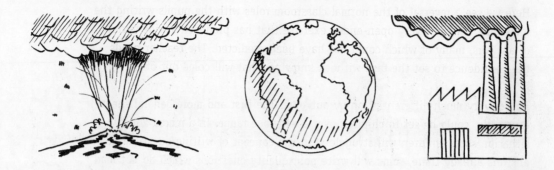

You are used to giving answers to questions set in a variety of ways. For some questions there is only one correct answer but on other occasions a number of responses are considered as being correct, even though some answers could be regarded as stronger than others. This exercise reverses the normal process by giving you the answer. Your task is to provide suitable questions. Try to give as many questions as possible to each of the answers that are listed. Look for both the obvious and the less obvious questions. These 'questions' could be in simple written form or presented as a diagram, puzzle or problem.

The answers

1   drainage basin
2   the main export
3   a heavily populated region
4   piedmont glacier
5   continental drift
6   very humid conditions
7   it is illegal
8   longshore drift
9   Köppen classification
10 oxbow lake
11 mackerel sky
12 magma
13 six-figure grid references
14 the importance of artificial satellites
15 because it is very fine grained
16 a grey colour
17 typhoon
18 permafrost

THE QUESTION IS

Teaching notes

Here we see a reversal of the normal classroom roles with the pupils writing the questions. This is a very open-ended exercise that has produced a wide variety of answers, many of which could not have been predicted. The teacher needs the confidence to set the task without knowing what will come out of it.

This is very much differentiation by outcome. The first and more general sheet, especially, could be set to children over a wide age range. In a mixed ability situation some children will struggle with the concept of writing questions to answers already there, some will write poor quality questions which do not lead to the answers from the information given. However many will understand what is required and will set questions which fit the criteria. Able children tend to exploit the situation best of all, providing amazing questions when they are given their freedom.

The original version stands in its own right but some teachers might be concerned about the content and its application. The science, history and geography versions show just how much this process can be linked to subject material. Indeed it can be narrowed down further to particular modules of work.

The sheets can be used directly but they also act as exemplars for teachers to write their own. If teachers do follow this route, one piece of advice is to mix up the complexity of the 'answers' and also to vary how specific or open that they are. This mix is likely to produce the best results - which are also most likely to occur where the class atmosphere encourages experimentation, openness and flexibility of response.

OR

Every situation or piece of evidence is open to a number of interpretations. Some explanations are more likely than others.

Look at the situations described below. Each has one interpretation with an invitation, provided by the word **OR**, for you to see how many others you can suggest. You may also indicate ways in which the various views could be tested in appropriate cases.

1   A bright light moving across the sky is an Unidentified Flying Object **OR** ...

2   A sore throat is the start of a cold **OR** ...

3   At the scene of a murder, traces of blood of group A were found. The murderer belongs to blood group A **OR** ...

4   You are waiting at the railway station for a friend who fails to arrive as expected. He/she has missed the train **OR** ...

5   Tommy has won the 100 metres race on the School Sports Day. He is the best runner in the school **OR** ...

6   A fire-engine seen rushing along a main road during a bad thunder-storm is going to a house struck by lightning **OR** ...

7   The record that reaches Number One in The Charts is the best record on sale at that time **OR** ...

8   During an investigation into a burglary a detective proved that a suspect was lying about his movements on a particular day. This showed that the suspect was guilty of the crime **OR** ...

9   Mr Still switched off his television just after a play started. Mr Still does not like plays **OR** ...

10 As a result of an appeal to help refugees after an earthquake, the Brown family donated £5 and the Hedge family gave £1. The Browns care for other people more than the Hedges do **OR** ...

11 Tom promised his wife, Susan, that he was not going to drink anymore. When Susan saw him coming out of a public house it was obvious that Tom had broken his promise **OR** ...

12 In the school examinations Margaret scored 72% in physics and 56% in geography. Margaret is a better physicist than a geographer **OR** ...

Now you might like to think up some more situations that have alternative interpretations, and which use the word **OR**.

OR

Teaching notes

An important feature of a skills curriculum for all children, and especially for the able, is that it allows individuality. We need to ask more open-ended questions to which there is more than one answer. Most situations are open to several interpretations. Some answers are stronger than others and a useful discussion can take place on the merits and weaknesses of the alternative views.

The situations used in **OR** play upon a number of themes.

Among these are:

1   Coincidence and looking beyond the obvious. A fire-engine called out in a thunderstorm may be going to a normal fire that has nothing to do with the weather.

2   Insufficient evidence, which needs extra information before a strong opinion can be given. A sore throat may very well herald a cold but it is also a symptom of many diseases and illnesses.

3   A straightforward explanation of something that seems strange. A bright light in the sky could be an aeroplane or a comet.

4   The question of comparability. Is 72% in physics automatically better than 56% in geography? Is an article that sells most necessarily the best? To what extent does winning one race on a particular day, over a specific distance, make an athlete the best?

5   Non-sequiturs. Because a suspect lies about one point does not mean that he is guilty of the crime under review.

WHO AM I?

When we are given pieces of information it is possible to work out new points by careful consideration of the original data. This process is known as deduction. Perhaps the most famous practitioner of the art of deduction is Sherlock Holmes. He has delighted readers by his ability to draw dramatic conclusions from clues and information.

Below there are descriptions of a number of people, written by themselves. You are asked to identify them - in other words to answer the question 'Who am I?' You may not be able to give a particular name but you should be in a position to suggest the nature of the person. The facts might fit a number of possibilities - if so give alternatives. Whatever suggestions you make it is important to back your views by close reference to the passages.

Person A

I enjoy all the attention most of the time but there are times when I wish I could go shopping without people making a fuss of me. Still, there aren't many people of my age who earn even a fraction of the money that I make in a year. My manager has been a great help - without him things would have been much more difficult. One of the great things is the travelling. So far I've been to France, Germany, Holland, Sweden and Italy.

Who am I?

Person B

There are tremendous pressures in my job and I get little time to relax with my family. Every day seems to bring a new problem, either at home or abroad. There never seems to be a dull moment. There are some difficult decisions to make.

Who am I?

Person C

The days' journeys were long and hard but what kept us going was the thought of the new life we had ahead of us. It was exciting but also rather awe-inspiring to think that we would be breaking new ground. We realised that there was danger and we took care to keep close formation.

Who am I?

WHO AM I?

Person D

It was odd to sit there in the dusk, thinking of the events that had brought me and thousands of others to this spot, so far from home. This was the calm before the storm. None of us knew what tomorrow would bring but we felt that life might never be the same again.

Who am I?

Person E

My training was long and hard but it was all worth it in the end. It is a good feeling to be in a position to help people when they most need assistance. There are very sad moments when you realise that you have failed despite all your efforts.

Who am I?

Person F

Many people tell me how envious they are that I am able to work at home. There seems to be a feeling that there is no real work involved, but I have to discipline myself or I would not make my deadlines. There are times when my study seems to be my prison!

Who am I?

Person G

How difficult it was when I first started work. There is much more machinery now and safety precautions are tighter. Too many of my workmates failed to reach their retirement. Output was all that mattered.

Who am I?

Person H

People are funny when they find out what I do for a living. I don't understand it - after all someone has to do the job.

Who am I?

Person I

Nobody likes to make mistakes but an error of judgement on my part has very serious consequences.

Who am I?

WHO AM I?

Person J

Most people think of my job as being glamorous and exciting but there is also a tremendous amount of hard repetitive work.

Who am I?

Person K

I suppose that mine is a funny kind of life, not really being myself.

Who am I?

Person L

What a strange mixture! I spend so much time waiting and then there are periods of intense activity.

Who am I?

Person M

Just be thankful that you are not me!

Who am I?

Person N

If only I had known what the results were going to be I would not have acted the way I did.

Who am I?

Person O

Everybody made such a fuss of me but what I did was very little really.

Who am I?

Person P

If only they had listened to me.

Who am I?

WHO AM I?

Teaching notes

Much work done by children is necessarily closed. It is helpful for able children in particular to have as many open-ended situations as possible. Then they are in a position to make an individual contribution.

Each of the people from A to P has valid alternative identities. The pupils must relate their answers to the data provided - it is not a case of 'anything goes'. This is good practice for many subject areas in encouraging relevance in answers and weighting evidence to inform the response. In history, for instance, a key skill is recognising the limits of evidence.

There is a deliberate pattern to the sections. Those at the beginning have more than one valid answer but the feasible replies are limited by the detail of the information. Person A is likely to suggest a fashion model, pop star, sports star etc. Person C is likely to have been involved in exploration or colonisation - perhaps he or she was part of a wagon train moving westwards across America.

The further the activity goes, the less detailed and specific is the information provided. There still needs to be a basic logic used to deduce from what is there, but the range becomes wider and more open. Person P - 'If only they had listened to me' - could be one of very many people but it must be someone involved in some kind of disaster or difficulty or problem.

Who Am I? does therefore link logical thinking and weighing evidence to produce a response, with an open-ended approach.

NOW YOU SEE IT

NOW YOU SEE IT

HAVE YOU SEEN SHADOWS ON THE WALL OR FLICKERING IN THE FLAMES
OF A FIRE AND ALLOWED YOUR IMAGINATION TO TURN THEM INTO
SHAPES AND PICTURES?

ARE YOU AN OBSERVANT PERSON WITH AN EYE FOR DETAIL? CAN YOU PICK
OUT AN INDIVIDUAL ITEM FROM A COMPLICATED WHOLE, HOWEVER MUCH
IT HAS BEEN OBSCURED?

This activity is an opportunity to explore both observation and imagination at the same time. You are presented with a sheet that is packed with illustrations. Some objects have been drawn in a straightforward manner. Elsewhere there are lines, patterns, and shapes that can be turned into figures with a little imagination.

Write down a list of both the obvious items and those that depend upon your own interpretation. To help you describe their positions there is a grid of letters and numbers that can be used. You may wish to write an account or story that links some of these items.

Look carefully and let your mind work upon the shapes and patterns.

NOW YOU SEE IT!

NOW YOU SEE IT

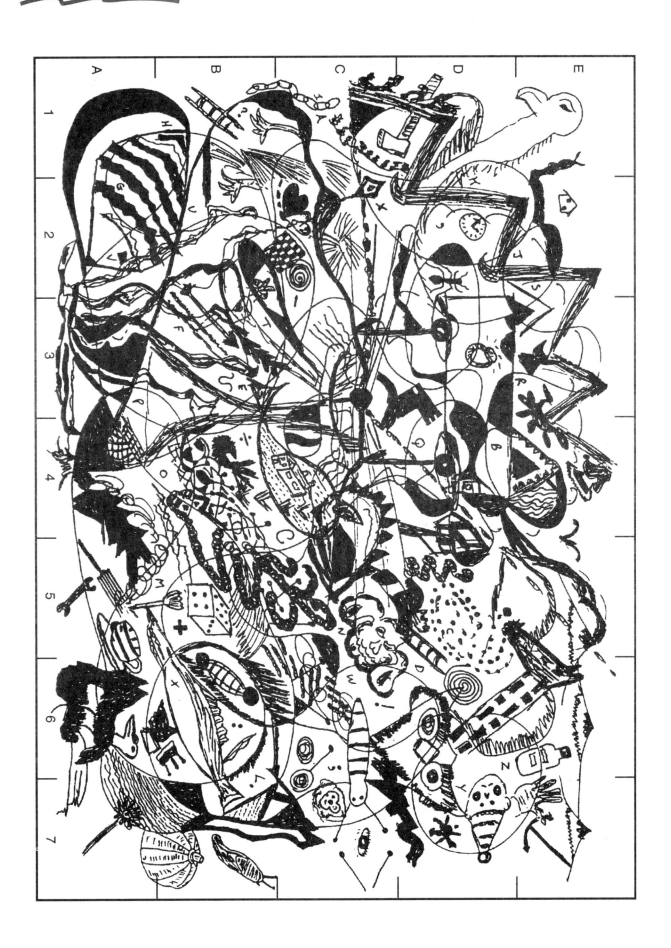

NOW YOU SEE IT

Teaching notes

This is a piece of work that encourages observation and imagination, two skills that form an interesting contrast. The illustration was put together by deliberately drawing in some small items, by creating larger shapes like the cat's head out of a disguised background and by adding lines, squiggles, scribbles and doodles. As a result children can identify items that have been included deliberately but they can also see shapes and figures that have occurred by accident. Moving the sheet round through 360° gives interesting new viewpoints.

Possible methods

1   The teacher may want the children to range over the illustration without guidance, identifying objects and creating shapes and pictures from their own imagination.

2   The picture can be divided into specific sections by means of the numbers 1 to 7 and the letters A to E. Thus you could ask the pupils to concentrate upon areas 6C, 3B and 7E, for instance. (To fit in with the practice used in mathematics, pupils should be encouraged to go horizontally first and then vertically).

3   For whatever work the teacher decides, sections could be selected by drawing out lots representing the different areas.

4   The sheet can be used for creative writing. If particular sections are designated, children could write a story using items from these areas, either obvious or from their interpretation of the shapes. This is an example of creativity within parameters. A combination of open-endedness and some limitations often produces interesting results.

5   Pupils could be asked to create their own sheet. It might be helpful to tease out the ways in which *Now You See It* has been created and what the various components are.

6   Some children might well enjoy the chance to create meaning from the sheet by interpreting parts of the picture, not just in terms of what they think they can see, but also in terms of what it might mean.

Personal interpretation is a valuable activity to encourage.

JUST IMAGINE

It is interesting to wonder what might happen if present circumstances changed in one way or another. Let your imagination run as you consider the following situations. Some of them are serious, while others are not so serious.

Just imagine...

1   that you woke up one morning and you could not see.

2   that a mysterious illness wiped out the fox population of Britain.

3   that mice grew to ten times their present size and developed a superior intelligence.

4   that glass had not been invented.

5   that it was made compulsory by law to vote in elections.

6   that sea water could be drunk without ill effects.

7   that you had the opportunity to bring back to life one person from the past.

8   that people could choose their own weather.

9   that a bruise never faded from the skin.

10 that cars could be run on water as fuel.

11 that human beings were incapable of walking more than one mile a day.

12 that it was no longer compulsory to go to school.

13 that, like Dr Dolittle, you had the power of communication with animals.

14 that anything rising above 10 metres from the ground was destroyed by changing atmospheric pressure (solid structures like buildings were not affected).

15 that there really was a 'Lost World' where dinosaurs still lived.

16 that it was always winter in the Northern Hemisphere.

17 that Hitler's Germany had carried out a successful invasion of Britain.

18 that human beings did not develop the power of speech until the age of six.

19 that you were given the opportunity to look into the future and see your own life ahead of you.

20 that you had the power to solve just one national or international problem.

Now, see if you can think up some other interesting situations that you could **just imagine**.

JUST IMAGINE

Teaching notes

Analysis is an important thinking skill. Imaginative thinking is a key component in many curriculum areas, especially for able children. *Just Imagine* combines the two in a cross-curricular piece of work. For each of the 'Just Imagines' included the children have to analyse and understand the context before allowing their imagination to run.

The varying situations each involve an existing position to be considered before imagining the change. If a mysterious illness wiped out the fox population of Britain there would be consequences for other animals and for human beings. The place of the fox in the food chain and the balance of the species would be important areas to investigate. A useful tool to use in this particular example, and many others in the list, would be that of Tony Buzan's mind mapping. A topic web with the fox at the centre would encourage an analysis of the different connections and relationships that could be affected. This visual interpretation is a preferred learning style for many children.

Many of the 'Just Imagines' have a strong element of evaluation. If you had the opportunity to bring back to life one person from the past, or you had the power to solve just one national or international problem, judgement and prioritisation would be important components of your decision-making.

Hypothesising is a key trigger word associated with synthesis. All these situations involve hypothetical thinking. Many necessitate looking for alternatives. If human beings were incapable of walking more than one mile a day, or did not develop the power of speech until the age of six, we would need to find alternative ways of moving or communicating.

The higher-order thinking skills are represented well in *Just Imagine*. Differentiation by outcome takes place because the work is open-ended. Responses are likely to be very varied and individual.

Contexts

Possible uses for this activity include:

❖ as a stimulus for general classroom discussion

❖ as the basis for a debate, taking a specific item and arguing whether it would be a good development or not

❖ as differentiated homework

❖ to generate a piece of creative writing by encouraging children to develop a story concerning the changes involved in a specific item

❖ to produce a visual outcome through topic webs that plot all the possible effects of a change

❖ as a piece of extension work, by fitting these or similar 'Just Imagines' to appropriate modules within a subject

❖ as an enrichment or extension item, by pupils creating their own 'Just Imagines' with, or without, an analysis of the likely consequences

Effective Resources for Able and Talented Children © Barry Teare (Network Educational Press, 1999)

The School Effectiveness Series focuses on practical and useful ideas for individual schools and teachers. The series addresses the issues of whole school improvement along with new knowledge about teaching and learning, and offers straightforward solutions that teachers can use to make life more rewarding for themselves and those they teach.

Book 1: *Accelerated Learning in the Classroom* by Alistair Smith
ISBN: 1-85539-034-5   £15.95
- The first book in the UK to apply new knowledge about the brain to classroom practice
- Contains practical methods so teachers can apply accelerated learning theories to their own classrooms
- Aims to increase the pace of learning and deepen understanding
- Includes advice on how to create the ideal enviroment for learning and how to help learners fulfil their potential
- Offers practical solutions on improving performance, motivation and understanding

Book 2: *Effective Learning Activities* by Chris Dickinson
ISBN: 1-85539-035-3   £8.95
- An essential teaching guide which focuses on practical activities to improve learning
- Aims to improve results through effective learning, which will raise achievement, deepen understanding, promote self-esteem and improve motivation
- Includes activities which are designed to promote differentiation and understanding
- Includes activities suitable for GCSE, National Curriculum, Highers, GSVQ and GNVQ

Book 3: *Effective Heads of Department* by Phil Jones & Nick Sparks
ISBN: 1-85539-036-1   £8.95
- Contains a range of practical systems and approaches; each of the eight sections ends with a 'checklist for action'
- Designed to develop practice in line with OFSTED expectations and DfEE thinking by monitoring and improving quality
- Addresses issues such as managing resources, leadership, learning, departmental planning and making assessment valuable
- Includes useful information for senior managers in schools who are looking to enhance the effectiveness of their Heads of Department

Book 4: *Lessons are for Learning* by Mike Hughes
ISBN: 1-85539-038-8   £11.95
- Brings together the theory of learning with the realities of the classroom environment
- Encourages teachers to reflect on their own classroom practice and challenges them to think about why they teach in the way they do
- Offers practical suggestions for activities that bridge the gap between recent developments in the theory of learning and the constraints in classroom teaching
- Ideal for stimulating thought and generating discussion

Book 5: *Effective Learning in Science* by Paul Denley and Keith Bishop
ISBN: 1-85539-039-6   £11.95
- Encourages discussion about the aims and purposes in teaching science and the role of subject knowledge in effective teaching
- Tackles issues such as planning for effective learning, the use of resources and other relevant management issues
- Offers help in the development of a departmental plan to revise schemes of work, resources, classroom strategies, in order to make learning and teaching more effective
- Ideal for any science department aiming to increase performance and improve results

Book 6: *Raising Boys' Achievement* by Jon Pickering
ISBN: 1-85539-040-X   £11.95
- Addresses the causes of boys' underachievement and offers possible solutions
- Focuses the search for causes and solutions on teachers working in the classroom
- Looks at examples of good practice in schools to help guide the planning and implementation of strategies to raise achievement
- Offers practical, 'real' solutions, along with tried and tested training suggestions
- Ideal as a basis for INSET or as a guide to practical activities for classroom teachers

Book 7: *Effective Provision for Able & Talented Children* by Barry Teare
ISBN: 1-85539-041-8   £11.95
- Basic theory, necessary procedures and turning theory into practice
- Main methods of identifying the able and talented
- Concerns about achievement and appropriate strategies to raise achievement
- The role of the classroom teacher, monitoring and evaluation techniques
- Practical enrichment activities and appropriate resources

Book 8: *Effective Careers Education & Guidance* by Andrew Edwards and Anthony Barnes
ISBN: 1-85539-045-0   £11.95
- Strategic planning of the careers programme as part of the wider curriculum
- Practical consideration of managing careers education and guidance
- Practical activities for reflection and personal learning, and case studies where such activities have been used
- Aspects of guidance and counselling involved in helping students to understand their own capabilities and form career plans
- Strategies for reviewing and developing existing practice

Book 9: *Best behaviour and Best behaviour FIRST AID* by Peter Relf, Rod Hirst,
Jan Richardson and GeorginaYoudell
ISBN: 1-85539-046-9   £12.95
- Provides support for those who seek starting points for effective behaviour management, for individual teachers and for middle and senior managers
- Focuses on practical and useful ideas for individual schools and teachers

Best behaviour FIRST AID
ISBN: 1-85539-047-7   £10.50 (pack of 5 booklets)
- Provides strategies to cope with aggression, defiance and disturbance
- Straightforward action points for self-esteem

Book 10: *The Effective School Governor* by David Marriott
ISBN 1-85539-042-6   £15.95 (including free audio tape)
- Straightforward guidance on how to fulfil a governor's role and responsibilities
- Develops your personal effectiveness as an individual governor
- Practical support on how to be an effective member of the governing team
- Audio tape for use in car or at home

Book 11: *Improving Personal Effectiveness for Managers* in Schools by James Johnson
ISBN 1-85539-049-3   £11.95
- An invaluable resource for new and experienced teachers in both primary and secondary schools
- Contains practical strategies for improving leadership and management skills
- Focuses on self-management skills, managing difficult situations, working under pressure, developing confidence, creating a team ethos and communicating effectively

Book 12: *Making Pupil Data Powerful* by Maggie Pringle and Tony Cobb
ISBN 1-85539-052-3   £12.95

- Shows teachers in primary, middle and secondary schools how to interpret pupils' performance data and how to use it to enhance teaching and learning
- Provides practical advice on analysing performance and learning behaviours, measuring progress, predicting future attainment, setting targets and ensuring continuity and progression
- Explains how to interpret national initiatives on data-analysis, benchmarking and target-setting, and to ensure that these have value in the classroom

Book 13: *Closing the Learning Gap* by Mike Hughes
ISBN 1-85539-051-5   £15.95

- Helps teachers, departments and schools to close the Learning Gap between what we know about effective learning and what actually goes on in the classroom
- Encourages teachers to reflect on the ways in which they teach, and to identify and implement strategies for improving their practice
- Helps teachers to apply recent research findings about the brain and learning
- Full of practical advice and real, tested strategies for improvement
- Written by a teacher, for teachers, to stimulate thought and interest 'at a glance'

Other Publications

Accelerated Learning in Practice by Alistair Smith
ISBN: 1-85539-048-5   £19.95

- The author's second book which takes Nobel Prize winning brain research into the classroom.
- Structured to help readers access and retain the information necessary to begin to accelerate their own learning and that of the students they teach.
- Contains over 100 learning tools, case studies from 36 schools and an up to the minute section.
- Includes 9 principles of learning based on brain research and the author's 7 Stage Accelerated Learning cycle.

Primary Publications

Imagine That... by Stephen Bowkett
ISBN: 1-85539-043-4   £19.95
- Hands-on, user-friendly manual for stimulating creative thinking, talking and writing in the classroom
- Provides over 100 practical and immediately useable classroom activities and games that can be used in isolation, or in combination, to help meet the requirements and standards of the National Curriculum
- Explores the nature of creative thinking and how this can be effectively driven through an ethos of positive encouragement, mutual support and celebration of success and achievement
- Empowers children to learn how to learn

Helping With Reading by Anne Butterworth and Angela White
ISBN: 1-85539-044-2   £14.95
- Includes sections on 'Hearing Children Read', 'Word Recognition' and 'Phonics'
- Provides precisely focused, easily implemented follow-up activities for pupils who need extra reinforcement of basic reading skills
- Activities which directly relate to the National Curriculum and 'Literacy Hour' group work. They are clear, practical and easily implemented. Ideas and activities can also be incorporated into Individual Education Plans
- Aims to address current concerns about reading standards and to provide support in view of the growing use of classroom assistants and parents to help with the teaching of reading

Please note that the prices given above are guaranteed until January 1st, 2000